REACTIONS TO SOCIAL AND ECONOMIC CHANGE 1750 - 1939

Edited by

Walter Minchinton

Professor of Economic History

University of Exeter

University of Exeter

1979

CONTENTS

PREFACE

The idea of research seminars in economic and social history emerged in the course of conversations with Tom Griffiths, the warden of the Devon Centre for Further Education at Dartington, who has continued to be a benevolent host. The first seminar was held in October 1967 and, as I write, the thirty-third has just been held. Of this total, 12 have been concerned with maritime history - this seminar has become an annual event - five with agriculture, three with social history, two each with urban and transport history while single seminars have been devoted to industrial history, labour history, vernacular architecture, population and mining history, the history of food marketing and of demand, capital formation and the entrepreneur.

The purpose of the seminars has been to bring together a variety of people interested in the particular topics - learned amateur historians, established academics, journalists, local enthusiasts, graduate students and others - to discuss the series of papers. I have always tried to cast my net as widely as possible and have had the ready co-operation of the archivists of the south-west, Peter Hull, Marjorie Rowe, Margaret Holmes and Ivor Collis, and of extra-mural tutors, particularly Fred Harris, Veronica Chesher, Bob Pim, Joe Bettey and Bob Machin, in trying to ensure that no one who could contribute or benefit should be left out. The membership of the Dartington seminars is not a closed society, it is an open one. And just as I am always ready to consider new topics or the repetition of old topics, provided the required number of suitable papers can be found, so I am always ready to welcome new participants. Anyone who would care to take part in one of these seminars has only to write to me expressing interest.

A second purpose of the seminars has been to provide a stimulus to research in a wide range of topics in local history and also to provide models of how topics can be tackled. In the informal format of the seminars, the amateur has the opportunity to seek advice of the professional both in the discussions and in face-to-face encounters over a pint of beer, a glass of sherry or a meal table. And such meetings have not only been effective but have led to a continuing exchange of information and ideas and to fruitful friendships. A third purpose has been to set the local problems in a wider context. Although a reviewer has recently reproved me for publishing general articles, I am completely unrepentant. The initial purpose of such general papers was to set the other papers given at the individual seminars in context. And this they effectively do in the published volumes. Moreover, in practical terms they serve to bring the other contents of the volumes to a wider audience. And no one is forced to publish in *Exeter Papers*. While my friends are happy that their efforts shall see the light of day in this form, I shall continue to publish them.

I have also been criticised for being vague about the meaning of the south-west. But this hardly seems a venal sin. Normally Devon and Cornwall, the 'parish' of the University of Exeter, will provide the core of the discussion but as a Bristolian by adoption, I see no reason why Somerset, Dorset, Wiltshire, Gloucestershire and now Avon should not come within the scope of this term.

And it may be advantageous, as with this volume, to range much more widely. The seminars are meant to provide for a fruitful exchange of scholarship; there is no reason why their scope should be cribbed and confined in a geographical straight-jacket. Nor will there be an attempt, as has been suggested, at balance. *Exeter Papers* is a continuing and open-ended series. Topics will be taken up as seems appropriate when a sufficient number of contributors can be gathered together.

Further, as I set out in the introduction to *Exeter Paper*, no. 11, for various reasons not all the papers have been published and no doubt this situation will continue to obtain. In consequence some issues have contained papers from individual seminars (as in this case) while others have brought papers contributed to two seminars between the same covers. Two considerations have determined such practice: an attempt to produce volumes of approximately the same length and at the same time to pursue a publishing programme of two numbers a year. And finally, incredible as it may seem since the statement has appeared on the back cover of every issue so far published, a reviewer has regretted that there is no general editor. He also suggests that individual editors were allowed to do as they liked. These statements come as much as a surprise to me as I am sure they will do to individual contributors and editors alike. For better or for worse, I intend to continue as the organiser of the seminars and the general editor of the series, encouraged both by the continuing support which the seminars receive and by the profitable sales of *Exeter Papers* themselves.

While the seminar at which the papers contained in this publication were given was called simply 'social history', a less vague title seemed appropriate for the published volume. It was not easy to decide on a suitable form of words to encompass all the papers here published but *Reactions to social and economic change, 1750-1939* indicates the essence of four of the papers and provides partial cover for the fifth, that by Norman Pounds.

In the past decade or so social history has been a burgeoning field and this volume reflects something of the range of interests. In the first paper Bob Bushaway well illustrates how folk ritual or customary activity was used by rural communities in the south of England in the century between 1750 and 1850 as a vehicle for social protest. Thus old forms were given new content in the context of changing conditions in the countryside. In analysing these events, Bushaway widens and deepens our understanding of reactions to social change.

David Gladstone's paper, which was given at very short notice due to the withdrawal of a speaker, is concerned with the care of the poor in Scotland and usefully sets the English situation in relief. Hitherto the 1845 Poor Law Amendment (Scotland) Act has been regarded primarily as a measure which removed the care of the poor from ecclesiastical control in response to pressure exerted, especially in the early 1840s, by representatives of the medical profession. But David Gladstone argues that the changes occurring within the Church itself - notably the successive splinterings of Presbyterianism of which the most extensive was the Disruption of 1843 - contributed considerably to the destruction of a nearly national system of social welfare and so to the amendment of the Scottish system of poor relief.

In his contribution, Adrian Vinson provides a case study of the kind of measures which were taken in a particular town, Southampton, to deal with the problem of unemployment. In a town where, because of the nature of work available, the situation was less severe than in the depressed areas dependant on the basic industries, Vinson well brings out the tensions in policy and practice which hampered the emergence of an effective solution. Unemployment divided, not united, the community. Whitehall and local council were at odds on administrative control and political accountability but most important, as Vinson concludes: the real dialogue was no longer between the respective merits of works and maintenance but between local rates and national taxes and between expenditure and economy - a dialogue in which, locally as nationally, financial orthodoxy had the loudest voice.

While Adrian Vinson deals with the institutional response, Peter Stead is concerned with the voluntary response to mass unemployment. With particular respect to South Wales, he argues that voluntary associations had a limited impact not only because resources were scarce but also because understanding of the real nature of the problem was limited. What the period really showed was that the unemployed, in Stead's words, not only asserted their independence but also established the reality of their own cultural existence. As a result unemployed clubs succeeded because they were taken over and moulded in the democratic image of their members; other schemes were either ignored or accepted without emotional commitment. And so the wheel comes full circle in this volume. In their different ways, Bushaway and Stead show the importance of the deep springs of community feeling in two rather different situations.

Finally, in a wide-ranging local study of the social structure of the Cornish town of Lostwithiel in the early nineteenth century, Norman Pounds shows, inter alia, how the geography of the growing town reflected the social structure. 42.8 per cent of its inhabitants found employment in craft industries, 21.2 per cent in agriculture and a further 12.4 per cent in mining while an almost similar percentage (11.7 per cent) were merchants, retailers and shopkeepers. And the population was mobile rather than static. In 1851 only 29.5 per cent of the men and 21.5 per cent of the women recorded in the census of that year had been born in the parish. He also shows how efforts were made in a Cornish town in the early nineteenth century to deal with what the twentieth century calls unemployment, a problem with which Stead and Vinson were also concerned.

In their different ways, ranging in time from the mid-eighteenth century almost to the mid-twentieth century and encompassing Cornwall, South Wales and Scotland as well as the south of England, these essays make their contribution to a discussion of differing reactions to economic and social change.

Walter Minchinton

CEREMONY, CUSTOM AND RITUAL: SOME OBSERVATIONS ON SOCIAL CONFLICT IN THE RURAL COMMUNITY, 1750-1850*

Robert W Bushaway

> Upon approaching the village towards 3 o'clock, I heard a good deal of uproar and tumult, intermingled at times with the heavy monotonous sound produced by blowing a cow's horn . . . I did not actually see the people by whom the noise was occasioned but took it for granted that it was one of those ebullitions of popular feeling which are sometimes occasioned in country villages, by a man's beating his wife, or other flagrant violation of the marriage vow.[1]

This account is taken from an anonymous pamphlet published at Oxford in 1830 entitled *Machine-breaking and the changes occasioned by it in the village of Turvey Down: a tale of the times*, a fictionalised description of the Captain Swing riots of the winter of 1830-1, written by someone who appeared to be well-acquainted both with the background to the disturbances and the form which they took. The author aimed to trace the causes of the riots and to show the futility of breaking agricultural machinery as a remedy. However, the quotation well illustrates the theme of this paper. The writer of the account mistook a machine-breaking riot for a gathering of 'rough music' - the common punishment for wife-beaters in the village community.[2] Here it is argued that organised forms of protest such as the Swing riots or the disturbances at Otmoor in Oxfordshire of the same year and some folk ceremonies and customs which show evidence of a strong conflict or protest element sprang from the same cultural experience and are consciously (in the sense of providing models for behaviour) or unconsciously inter-related.

Folklore can be looked upon as an unwritten moral code for the community, indicating what is tolerated, censuring what is not and acting as a vehicle for enforcing the collective will. In these last two it is clearly a form of social protest in itself. Transgressors of this morality, which might be termed a recognised code of behaviour, are made to feel the force of its sanctions, whilst its supporters are permitted to enjoy the rewards that are reciprocally theirs. In most cases these benefits amount to the recognition of due status or strength during the normal functioning of the community. It is in this way that the Italian Marxist, Antonio Gramsci, recommended the study of folklore as a legitimate and indeed indispensible method of understanding the structure of society, with its tensions and its conflicts. He wrote:

* I would like to thank Dr J G Rule and Mr F C Mather for their helpful comments.

1 *Machine-breaking and the changes occasioned by it in the village of Turvey Down: a tale of the times* (anonymous, about 1830); reprinted in *The rising of the agricultural labourers: nine pamphlets and six broadsides, 1830-31* (British Labour Struggles series, New York: Arno Press, 1972) p. 20.

2 For a full account of 'rough music' see Edward P Thompson, '"Rough music" - le charivari Anglais', *Annales*, 27 (1972) 285-312.

> We can say that to date folklore has been studied mainly as something 'picturesque' (in fact, to date, only erudite material has been gathered and the science of folklore has consisted mainly in the study of methods of collection, selection and classification of such material, that is, in the study of cautious practices and empirical principles which are necessary for the fruitful development of a particular aspect of erudition) . . . We must study it, instead, as a 'view of the world and of life', in great measure implicit, of certain strata (determinate in space and time) of society, in opposition (here, too, mostly implicit, mechanical, objective) to the 'official views of the world', (or, in a wider sense, of the cultured parts of a particular society) that has occurred throughout history's development.[1]

Furthermore, Gramsci considered more explicitly the profound nature of folklore as a form of popular morality:

> It is also true that there exists a 'popular morality', understood as a certain whole (in space and time) of maxims of practical conduct and customs which are derived from it or have produced it, . . . There exist imperatives which are much stronger, more tenacious and more effectual than those of official 'morality'.[2]

The confrontation between folklore and what Gramsci described as the 'official views of the world' inevitably produces conflict. It is in this way that the study of the operation of folklore can indicate to the historian some forms of conflict within the community. These observations can be usefully applied to an analysis of custom and ritual in eighteenth-century rural life.

The process of agricultural change in that century had profound consequences for the rural community. It has been asserted that as farming became more profitable, because of improved techniques, and farmers grew more wealthy, they became increasingly more status-conscious and, as Cobbett constantly lamented, sought to emulate the style of living of the genteel, distancing themselves from the lives and experiences of their labourers. Enclosure deprived the labouring community of much of the traditional economic basis of their lives, denying them sources of fuel and grazing for their beasts, as well as many marginal 'hedge-row' benefits, such as the gathering of nuts, wild fruits and plants. Fencing-off the commons and wastes and transforming them into farming land denied the labourers their traditional recreational areas. Therefore, as the farmers and landowners began to adopt attitudes associated with the development of the market economy, such as stricter definitions and control of rights of private property; so the labouring community, increasingly under pressure, defended traditional society and aggressively brandished their customs and ceremonies as a weapon in that defence. This albeit oversimplified and brief exposition of rural social change in the hundred years before 1850, goes some way to explain why the maintenance of folk customs and

1 Alastair Davidson, *Antonio Gramsci: the man, his ideas* (Australian New Left Review Publication, 1968) p. 86.

2 Davidson, *Gramsci*, p. 87.

practices provided a strong focus of conflict. A confrontation took place between the traditional view of social responsibilities and obligations on the one hand and the changing attitudes of the farmers towards work discipline which placed customary practices in a less favourable light, on the other.

Having briefly suggested why tension should have existed in the eighteenth-century rural community and why folk customs should have acted as a focus for that tension, I should like to illustrate in closer detail some elements of conflict which can be distinguished in the operation of harvest work. The in-gathering of the crop which was the culmination of the agricultural year, was woven round with a complex mesh of custom and ritual concerning both the organisation of the labour force, its payments and customary rewards, as well as the act of cutting, binding and carrying home the last sheaf and the last load. Harvest was of crucial importance to the labourers and their families, who were able, for this one occasion of the year, to enforce the traditional pattern of responsibilities and dues binding together farmer and labourer and to reaffirm the strength of this bond through the legitimation of custom. Farmers, in most cases, were obliged to accept their conditions, because without such acceptance, the labourers were unlikely to co-operate in the task.

Firstly, I would like to consider in some detail the in-gathering of the harvest, concentrating on some ritual elements symbolic of what might be called community solidarity and also the customary organisational factors. From this, the conflict between farm workers and farmers which developed during the period can be better understood. The precise details varied from place to place and from region to region; however, I shall concentrate on material relating to the south of England for the most part and in particular the county of Devon.

It was customary in southern England (as elsewhere in Britain) for the harvesters to elect one from among their number to act as leader or foreman. He was known as the 'lord' and his functions have been described thus:

> To him all the rest were required to give precedence, and to leave all transactions respecting their work. He made terms with the farmers for mowing, for reaping, and for all the rest of the harvest work; he took the lead with the scythe, with the sickle, and on the 'carrying days', he was to be first to eat, and the first to drink at all their refreshments, his mandate was to be law to all the rest who were bound to address him as 'my lord', and to show him all due honour and respect. Disobedience in any of these particulars was punished by imposing fines according to a scale previously agreed on by the 'lord' and all his vassals. In some instances, if any of his men swore or told a lie in his presence, a fine was imposed.[1]

In addition, the 'lord of the harvest' ensured the quality of the harvest work, fining those labourers who were slow, ill-disciplined or whose work was shoddy. In short, by common agreement amongst the

1 Robert Chambers, ed. *The book of days: a miscellany of popular antiquities* (London and Edinburgh, 1888) II, 376.

harvest men, the lord acted as leader and as negotiator between themselves and the farmer who had hired them.

Quite how widespread was the practice of electing a harvest lord cannot be estimated with any degree of certainty. As with most customary behaviour, much of the evidence is qualitative. Most sources refer to specific occurences or to general localities, using such phrases as 'in the surrounding neighbourhood' or 'in the immediate vicinity' when speaking of the distribution of folk practice. Therefore, at least for the period under consideration, a quantitative approach must be ruled out as being impractical. However, the practice of nominating a lord to negotiate terms and organise labour was durable enough to be recorded much later in the century in Flora Thompson's Oxfordshire.[1]

The harvest lord's significance for the study of some aspects of rural conflict lies in its emphasis on the elements of strength and status. The farmer would have found it difficult to impose such a strict form of work discipline upon the harvest labourers. The acknowledgement of the lord's position as a kind of Captain provides the historian with one possible organisational model for later movements of protest.

During harvest, food and drink were supplied as part of the contract which the lord made with each farmer. Also, a harvest-home supper was expected as part of that bargain.[2] Boisterous behaviour, familiarity and even a kind of insubordination which the less charitable farmers regarded as rank insolence was common. The gathering of harvest reassured the labouring poor of the continued relevance of traditional social values and the reciprocal relationship between sections of the village. Its rituals were potent as symbols of the solidarity of the community.

At the conclusion of harvest, the custom of 'crying the neck' was generally adhered to, particularly in Devon. One commentator described the custom in a letter to the antiquary, John Brand, in 1805:

> When the cutting of the wheat is finished a group or handful of the best ears is selected and being bound together forms what is called the neck. As soon as it is prepared the whole Band of Harvest People and in general all the Household, Master, Mistress, and children, and servants repair to the highest part of the farm; where one of them who possesses the best lungs and clearest voice, advancing before the rest of the Party and holding up the neck with both hands to the fullest extent of his reach commences the following cry or shout, in which he is instantly joined by everyone present.

1 'With no idea that they were at the end of a long tradition, they still kept up the old country custom of choosing as their leader the tallest and most highly skilled man amongst them, who was then called "King of the Mowers". For several harvests in the 'eighties they were led by the man known as Boamer. He had served in the Army and was still a fine, well-set-up young fellow with flashing white teeth and a skin darkened by fiercer than English suns' (Flora Thompson, *Lark rise to Candleford* (Oxford UP, 1973) p. 257).

2 See Eugene Aram, 'The Melsupper and shouting the churn' in *The genuine account of the life and trial of Eugene Aram for the murder of Daniel Clark* (London, 1759) p. 59.

A . . . . neck
We . . . . ha'en (have it)
God . . . . sa'en (save it)[1]

This cry culminated in a series of whoops and loud cheering. The ritual was important to the labourers, not because of any ancient memory or survival of the worship of some pagan earth-mother but because it reflected the co-operation between master and men and reinforced, at least for another year, the sense of community prevailing in the village. Group unity and the preservation of the traditional patterns of behaviour underlay other customs. For example, the ceremony of wassailing the apple tree, which usually took place on Twelfth Night, when a similar scene was enacted in the farmer's orchard and the elements of symbolic recitation and commensality were again present.[2] Conflict developed over adherence to such customs because the labourers confronted the farmers in the aggressive, dominant role of leader in the proceedings. 'Crying the neck' and wassailing the apple trees acted as a vehicle for the maintenance of the labourers' conception of traditional society, with its emphasis upon community, responsibility and obligation. They clung tenaciously to these rituals and were often far from deferential in their observance.[3] However, many of the more 'respectable' people of rural society were no longer on the side of the labourers and traditional moral behaviour. They sought to break away from the constraints of such time-consuming, expensive, unruly and insubordinate practices, seeing folk activities as an abuse of personal privilege and private property.

Elsewhere in England during the eighteenth century, the custom of claiming 'largess' was prevelant. Largess was an additional form of levy claimed by the harvesters from neighbouring farmers and the more wealthy houses in the community as a contribution to their celebrations which accompanied the successful completion of work. This money was collected in the same way that 'Christmas boxes' were demanded by tradesmen and apprentices in eighteenth-century towns, and indeed continue to be collected by those who provide services in modern society.[4] Joseph Haslewood described one such visitation as it occurred in Hertfordshire, making clear the implications of any refusal to contribute largess. He observed that:

> a deputation from the men usually traverse the neighbourhood and pray, at the different houses of respectability, largess. On the 30th August, 1819, I was at Broxbourne at a

1 British Library (BL), Additional Mss 41313, f. 86. This is a letter from Robert Studley Vidal to John Brand, dated Cornborough (Devon), 28 September 1805.

2 For accounts of apple tree wassailing see John Brand, *Observations on popular antiquities*, ed. Henry Ellis (London, 1813) I, 28. Also, Walter Minchinton, 'Cider and folklore', *Folklife*, XIII (1977) 66-79.

3 BL, Add Mss 41313, f. 85.

4 On Christmas boxes and opposition to the custom see a newspaper cutting affixed before the title page in Thomas Park's copy of John Brand's *Observations on popular antiquities* (Newcastle upon Tyne, 1777) in the British Library (810.e.4).

> gentleman's house and while sitting after dinner the servant entering said 'There was farmer --------- man to beg largess'. As I knew my friend had little if any arable land, I enquired where the farmer lived and found at Hoddesdon. The largess was in this instance refused but I found my friend gave to the servants of two or three farmers whose land lay immediately adjacent to his own and it seems possible that the custom has been founded on the propriety, if not necessity, of giving such men what we should call civility money and thereby prevent little infringements or a wanton despoiling of hedges, herbage etc.[1]

The use of the term 'civility money' indicates Haslewood's much deeper comprehension of the nature of folk customs than those who saw them as quaint and picturesque vestiges of bygone days which provided harmonious yet relatively harmless amusement. In this instance deference was a commodity which it was necessary for the farmer to buy, if he was to avoid expressions of popular displeasure.

Some farmers would not be intimidated and the conflict over traditional practices such as those associated with the gathering of harvest led to their slow but steady decline. However, only large-scale mechanisation at the end of the nineteenth century could totally root out the old ways, despite the disapproval and active hostility of many farmers. The following unsympathetic communication by a Devon farmer to the *Gentleman's Magazine* in 1816 illustrates both the opposition to harvest customs and also the chasm which had developed between the labourer and his master.

> The reaping and harvesting of the wheat in the county of Devon is attended with so heavy an expence, and with practices of so very disorderly a nature, as to call for the strongest mark of disapprobation, and their immediate discontinuance, or at least a modification of their pastime after the labours of the day. The wheat being ready to cut down, and amounting to from ten to twenty acres, notice is given in the neighbourhood that a reaping is to be performed on a particular day, when, as the farmer may be more or less liked in the village, on the morning of the day appointed a gang consisting of an indefinite number of men and women assemble in the field and the reaping commences after breakfast, which is seldom over till between eight and nine o'clock. This company is open for additional hands to drop in, at any time before the twelfth hour, to partake of the frolick of the day. By eleven or twelve o'clock the ale and cider has so much warmed and elevated their spirits, that their noisy jokes and ribaldry are heard to a considerable distance, and often serve to draw auxillary force within the accustomed time. The dinner, consisting of the best meat and vegetables, is carried into the fields between twelve and one o'clock; this is distributed with copious draughts of ale and cider; and by teo o'clock the pastime of cutting and binding the wheat is resumed, and continued without other interruption than the squabbles of the

1 Joseph Haslewood's copy of John Brand's *Observations on popular antiquities*, ed. Henry Ellis (London, 1813) (BL, 142.4.1,2) contains his own interleaved manuscript notes. For largess, see the note in Vol. I between pp. 447 and 448.

> party, until about Five o'clock, when what is called the drinkings are taken into the field, and under the shade of a hedge-row or a large tree, the panniers are examined, and buns, cakes and all such articles are found as the confectionary skill of the farmer's wife could produce for gratifying the appetites of her customary guests at this season. After the drinkings are over, which generally consume from half to three quarters of an hour (and even longer if such can be spared from the completion of the field) the amusement of the wheat-harvest is continued with such exertions as draw the reaping and binding of the field together with the close of the evening; this done, a small sheaf is bound up and set upon the top of one of the ridges, when the reapers retiring to a certain distance, each throws his reap-hook at the sheaf until one more fortunate, or less inebriated than the rest, strikes it down. This achievement is accompanied with the utmost stretch and power the voices of the company, uttering words very indistinctly, but somewhat to this purpose - 'We ha Yn! We ha Yn!' concluding with a horrid yell resembling a war-hoop of the Indian savages, which noise and tumult continue for about half an hour, when the company retire to the farmhouse to supper; which being over, large portions of ale and cider enable them to carouse and vociferate until two or three o'clock in the morning. At the same house, or that of a neighbouring farmer, a similar scene is renewed, beginning between eight and nine o'clock in the morning following, and so continued through the precious season of the wheat-harvest in this country. It must be observed, that the labourers thus employed in reaping, receive no wages; but in lieu therof they have an invitation to the farmer's house, to partake of a harvest frolic, and at Christmas also, during the whole of which time, and which seldom continues less than four or five days, the house is kept open night and day to the guests, whose behaviour during the time may be assimilated to the frolics of a bear-garden.[1]

The attack on some rural customs arose partly from the farmer's view of their costliness and indiscipline but it must not be overlooked that as such folk activity resolutely defended a form of popular morality, opposition to their continuance was not solely concerned with expense. Using Gramsci's view of the relevance of folklore for the study of society, the historian is able to observe a conflict between traditional and 'official' morality. The governors of village life sought to bring the threatening gestures of popular culture under control.

Opposition to folk activity because it represented and, indeed, defended traditional morality, as well as showed the labourers acting under their own initiative, can be identified as one level of social conflict. However, some customs and ceremonies in themselves embodied a strong element of confrontation. Social anthropologists tell us that certain rituals in which conflict between groups is a central feature and in which disruptive or anti-social behaviour is tolerated, can be interpreted as a demonstration of strength and importance, by

1 George L Gomme, *Extracts from the 'Gentleman's Magazine' on manners and customs* (London, 1885) pp. 45-6.

what might be regarded as 'weak' groups in the normal social hierarchy.[1] These rituals seem to occur when these groups feel threatened or are under some external pressure. Therefore, it is common to find ritual demonstrations of strength at certain times of the year when deprivation threatened, was at its worst or was soon to disappear. It would seem that the English rural community exhibited a similar pattern of ceremonial activity in the eighteenth century, when the labouring poor sought to demonstrate their strength or assert their importance. Such life-crisis rites of passage were observed during the months before Christmas, at Epiphany and on May day.

William Howitt, writing in the 1840s about the steady decline of folk custom, described Plough Monday ceremonies and their disruptive elements:

> The insolence of these Plough-bullocks as they are called, which might accord with ancient licence, but does not at all suit modern habits, has contributed more than anything else to put them down.[2]

The plough-bullocks, to which he referred, was the name applied to teams of labourers who went in procession from house to house on Plough Monday, the first Monday after Epiphany, in some areas of the Midlands. Llewellyn Jewitt recorded these gatherings much later in the century when they were no longer common, in Derbyshire:

> On Plough Monday, the 'Plough-bullocks' are still occasionally seen; they consist of a number of young men from various farm-houses, who are dressed up in ribbands, their shirts (for they wear no coats or undercoats) literally covered with rosettes of various colours, and their hats bound round with ribbands, and decorated with every kind of ornament that comes in their way; these young men yoke themselves to a plough, which they draw about, preceeded by a band of music, from house to house collecting money; they are accompanied by the fool and Bessy; the fool being dressed in the skin of a calf, with the tail hanging down behind, and Bessy, generally a young man in female attire, covered with a profusion of ribbands and other meretricious finery. The fool carries an inflated bladder tied to the end of a long stick, by way of a whip, and which he does not fail to apply pretty soundly to the heads and shoulders of his team; to these personages are usually two or three more drivers, armed with similar bladders, and a ploughman and attendants. When anything is given, a cry of largess is raised, and a dance performed around the plough; but if a refusal to their application for money is made, they not unfrequently plough up the pathway, door stone, or any other portion of the premises that happen to be near.[3]

1 See Victor W Turner, *The ritual process* (Routledge & Kegan Paul, 1969) for a discussion of this view.

2 William Howitt, *The rural life of England* (London, 1840) p. 471.

3 Frederick W Llewellyn Jewitt, 'On ancient customs and sports of the county of Derby', *Journal of the British Archaeological Society*, VII (1851) 201-2.

The sanction of ploughing-up the property of ungenerous neighbours was present in the ceremony a century earlier as the following account confirms:

> On this day *[Plough Monday]* the young men yoke themselves and draw a plough about with musick, and one or two persons in antic dresses like Jack-Puddings, go from house to house to gather money to drink. If you refuse them, they plough up your dunghill.[1]

The original purpose of these visits was to solicit money for the upkeep of the 'plough light' in the parish church but after the Reformation the money collected by the men was spent on drink and festivity. The more respectable inhabitants were increasingly reluctant to permit such behaviour. Howitt noted:

> In some places I have known them enter houses, whence they could only be ejected by the main power of the collected neighbours; for they extended their excursions often to a distance of ten miles or more, and where they were the most unknown, there practised the most insolence. Nobody regrets the discontinuence of this usage.[2]

Such activity was far from deferential and it is interesting to note the concentration upon largess and the threat of abuse of property or person for those who did not comply with their requests.

In the counties of southern England, Plough Monday was apparently not observed with the same degree of aggression. Yet other ceremonies can be found which embody the central elements of the soliciting of charitable doles and the sanction of damage to property for non-compliance. The custom of lent-crocking was common in the eighteenth and nineteenth centuries, particularly in Dorset, Wiltshire and Devon. On Shrove Tuesday, parties of youths went from house to house soliciting pancakes or other food, drink or money contributions. At any house where such bounty was not forthcoming, they exacted a violent penalty. Retiring to some distance, the boys subjected the front door of the house to a shower of broken crockery, to the annoyance of the inhabitants. It would seem that the original customary format depended to some extent on the skill of the boys, who, if they were able, tried to reach the kitchen undetected and place a piece of china on the table, thereby entitling themselves to demand a reward. If they were detected the pancakes were not given. Access was given by leaving the front door upon the latch. By the early nineteenth century the intricacy of the custom had disappeared, perhaps because of the declining support of householders. The sanction of showering the door with sherds became the custom's dominant feature. In one account of the custom as it prevailed in some parts of Devon, other motives are made apparent. Lent-crocking, it was observed:

> appears to be now persisted in from no other motive than that of insulting and annoying many of the most peaceable and deserving inhabitants of the neighbourhood. In fact, it at present takes

1 *Gentleman's Magazine*, December 1762. Cited in William Carew Hazlitt, *Faiths and folklore of the British Isles* (2 vols, London, 1905; New York: Benjamin Blom, 1965) p. 496.

2 Howitt, *Rural life*, p. 472.

> no other character than that of a sorry despicable method which the most worthless and disorderly of the rabble use to express their dislike and hatred of those who least resemble themselves; and consists in throwing a quantity of potsherds and filth into the principal Passage of the House; or if the door be secured, in dashing materials of this description against it with such vehemence as not unfrequently to break it or otherwise injure it so as to render a new one necessary.[1]

This is how the custom was observed in some Devon towns by Robert Studley Vidal in 1805, where the idea of soliciting pancakes was done away with, the crowd merely being content to damage the doors of respectable inhabitants. In the neighbouring villages, the custom retained its original purpose, although the sanction of crocking was still an integral part of the observance. Vidal continued:

> The heaving . . . at the door of the House from where nothing could be obtained, was probably designed to show that the owner was a person so inhospitable, so destitute of common charity, as to refuse even a Pancake to the Poor on Shrove Tuesday.

He also commented that the ungenerous inhabitant had to endure for the rest of the year:

> the notion of scandal and disgrace which the Common people annex to anyone's having Potsherds thrown at his Door at this particular Season.[2]

In Dorset, where lent-crocking prevailed until the end of the nineteenth century, it was reported that the throwing of potsherds at people's doors was acceptable but that youths were not allowed to throw stones. Various rhymes have been noted which were chanted by the assembly, the following verse coming from Milton Abbey during the latter half of the century.

> Please I've come a-shroving
> For a piece of pancake
> Or a little ruckle cheese
> Of your own making
> If you don't give me some,
> If you don't give none,
> I'll knock down your door
> With a great marrow bone
> And away I'll run.

This was no idle threat, as the account continued that 'in this way real damage was done'.[3] However, the custom was gradually brought under control by the increased exercise of the law. A report in the

1 BL, Add Mss 41313, f. 80. A letter from Robert Studley Vidal to John Brand, dated 10 July 1805.

2 BL, Add Mss 41313, f. 81.

3 John Symonds Udal, *Dorsetshire folklore* (Hertford: S Austin & Sons, 1922) pp. 24-5.

Bridport News in the 1880s described a visit made by a party of lent-crockers on the house of a widow. Receiving no pancakes, they pelted the door with sherds and damaged it in the process. The case was brought to court and:

> The Bench thought that sufficient evidence had been given to prove guilt, and fined the defendents six shillings and costs, as well as ordering them to pay eight shillings damages. After some protest the money was paid.[1]

Customary action, therefore, often legitimated unruly behaviour, at least for most of the period under discussion, and at certain crisis points in the life cycle of the rural community, the labouring poor felt compelled to make a demonstration of strength to defend their conception of traditional morality, based upon the principles of obligation and responsibility. In some circumstances this process was dramatically modified and adapted for the defence of specific community rights, in direct defiance of the landowning or governing interest. At Great Wishford in Wiltshire, a remarkable custom of this kind can be found. Since at least as early as the beginning of the seventeenth century complex ceremony was used to defend a popular custom. The inhabitants of Great Wishford claimed a right to gather dead wood (commonly called 'snapping wood') throughout the year, in Grovely Forest which was the property of the Pembroke family. These rights were set down in a charter of 1603 which is still preserved in the parish church.[2] In order to confirm this right, annually on Oak Apple Day (29 May) the inhabitants marched to the forest to cut green boughs, with which they decorated the church and their houses. For most of the eighteenth century, they then processed to Salisbury, where the right was reaffirmed in the cathedral with the cry of 'Grovely, Grovely, and all Grovely'. Afterwards there followed a small fair on the cathedral green with booths and stalls. This was discontinued early in the following century, probably because the cathedral authorities objected to the fair, and the ceremony was confined to Great Wishford. Several attempts were made by the Pembrokes to challenge the right and at one point in the seventeenth century it was commuted by general agreement to a charitable allowance. Barford St Martin, another village bordering on Grovely Forest and with similar claims to those of Great Wishford, never regained the right to dead wood and settled for an annual allowance of coal, distributed at Christmas. Yet, by some means, the inhabitants of Wishford began again to claim the right of gathering snapping wood and defended their action by adhering to the unusual ritual demonstration on Oak Apple Day. Other attempts to suppress the custom in the nineteenth century failed and the ceremony continued until the Oak Apple Club was founded in 1892 as a permanent organisation to preserve the rights of Wishford and to oversee the annual procession. Despite the opposition of the Lord of the Manor at various times in the two centuries before the foundation of the Club, the inhabitants of Great Wishford proclaimed their customary right to gather wood in Grovely Forest and defended that right through the elaboration of annual ritual. The ceremony itself

1 Udal, *Dorsetshire folklore*, p. 26.

2 See Edwin H Steele, *The history of oak apple day in Wishford magna* (Salisbury, 1951) which gives an account of the ceremony and a copy of the original charter. Also Edith Olivier, *Wiltshire* (Robert Hale, 1951) pp. 242-9.

was probably borrowed from other May observances, forms of which were quite common throughout southern England. The peculiar adaptation of these ceremonies in the defence of the collective right of gathering wood at Great Wishford, demonstrates how, in some cases, ceremony could be utilised as a legitimating factor.

The months of November and December were very significant to the labouring poor. Harvest earnings were exhausted and work was scarce at what was traditionally a slack period in the farming cycle. The clustering of several 'doleing' customs in the weeks preceding Christmas was a reflection of this pressure. One custom which took place on St Andrew's day (30 November) embodied a strong protest element and again took the form of a collective demonstration of strength. The diversion of 'squirrel hunting' was common in several places in southern England on this day. At Easling in Kent:

> the labourers and the lower kind of people, assembling together, form a lawless rabble, and being accoutred with guns, poles, clubs, and other such weapons, spend the greatest part of the day in parading through the woods and grounds with loud shoutings; and, under the pretence of demolishing the squirrels, some few of which they kill, they destroy numbers of hares, pheasants, partridges, and in short whatever comes their way, breaking down hedges, and doing much other mischief, and in the evening betaking themselves to the ale-houses, finish their career there as is usual with such sort of gentry.[1]

The custom of 'St Andr'ng' was also kept up, in similar fashion, in parts of Sussex until the early nineteenth century when stricter protection of game and further enclosure of coppices led to its discontinuence.[2] There, as in Kent, the primary aim was to do damage to fences and hedges and to take game. The assembled crowd directed their actions against the preserves of propertied men, mapped out in the Acts of Enclosure and protected by the increasingly severe game laws. Research has not yet uncovered earlier reference to the custom in the particular form recorded for the period under analysis, although squirrel hunting was widespread as an amusement throughout much of southern England, especially in the New Forest.[3] Ceremony and social conflict were intermixed in the practice of 'St Andr'ng' in a way which throws different light on the view that there was little popular protest against enclosure.

At Duffield in Derbyshire, the squirrel hunt took place on Wakes Monday and the right of gathering wood was preserved by collective action not dissimilar to but more implicit than Wishford's practice. Llewellyn Jewitt recounted that:

1 Brand, *Observations*, I, 323.

2 Frederick E Sawyer, 'Sussex folk-lore and customs connected with the seasons', *Sussex Archaeological Collections*, XXXIII (1883) 253.

3 See D H Moutray Read, 'Hampshire folklore', *Folklore*, XXII (1911) 323-4; John R Wise, *The New Forest: its history and scenery* (London, 1863) p. 182.

> The young men of the village assemble together on the Wakes Monday, each provided with a horn, a pan, or something capable of making a noise, and proceed to Kedleston Park, where with shouting and the discordant noise of the instruments, they frighten the poor little squirrels until they drop from the trees. Several having been thus captured, the hunters return to Duffield, and having released the squirrels amongst some trees re-commence the hunt. At the same place, the right of collecting wood in the forest is singularly observed, - for the young men in considerable number collect together, and having taken possession of any cart they can find, yoke themselves to it, and proceeded by horns, remove any trees or other wood from the various lanes and hedge-rows; this is done almost nightly between September and the Wakes, in the first week in November, when a huge bonfire is made of the wood collected, on the Wakes Monday.[1]

The central elements of the invasion of private property and the disorderly behaviour of the crowd were present at Duffield, although less explicitly than in the proceedings in Kent and Sussex. This, perhaps, was the reason for the survival of the custom until a later date in Derbyshire. The activities of the crowd were less destructive and less obviously directed against rural privilege.

The folk, therefore, were not only tenacious in the conflict over customs and ceremonies but found in some of them a vehicle for protest against the destruction of traditional society and, indeed, a legitimating agent in their defence of some collective rights which were in danger of being revoked. Custom permitted excesses and affronts at times when economic pressure was great and in some areas restrained the farmers' freedom to organise his labourers and pay them as he thought fit. A pattern of folk activity emerges which, for the eighteenth century and part of the nineteenth century, was robust, aggressive, demanding and far from deferential. Traditional society with its emphasis upon reciprocal dues and responsibilities was being challenged by the emergence of social thinking more attuned to the needs and requirements of the market economy; in response folklore was used by the labouring community as a weapon in the ensuing conflict.

It is not surprising to find that a similar pattern can be deduced in more orthodox movements of social protest. Historians are well aware of ritual and ceremonial forms in such movements. The study of food riots in the eighteenth century has demonstrated the widespread use of symbols of protest, ritual rough handling of the enemies of traditional society and the parading of effigies.[2] The activities of Rebecca and her followers in Wales, also embodied much ritual behaviour, inspired by the Welsh folk experience.[3] Ceremonial activity, accompanying

1 Jewitt, 'On ancient customs', pp. 208-9.

2 See Edward P Thompson, 'The moral economy of the English crowd in the eighteenth century', *Past and Present*, No. 50 (February 1971) 76-136.

3 See David Williams, *The Rebecca Riots: a study in agrarian discontent* (Cardiff: University of Wales Press, 1953). See also 'Rebecca', *Quarterly Review*, LXXIV (1844) 225-7.

popular disturbance, had more significance for the participants than merely the preservation of their anonymity or the addition of a sense of drama to the proceedings. By examining some events which occurred during the Captain Swing riots in the winter of 1830-1, I hope to demonstrate that a pattern of folk activity not dissimilar to much of the ceremonial experience of the rural labouring poor, asserted itself, both because it acted in some cases as a model for behaviour and because the motive of the defence of traditional morality lay at the roots of both forms of action. We are, in a sense, not looking at two distinctive types of collective behaviour but at similar phenomena. Folklore and social conflict were inter-related in the activities of Captain Swing and his adherents not in a picturesque way but in opposition to the 'official views' of the relationship between groups in the community.

The riots, or 'mobbings' as they were known colloquially, in 1830 were an attempt by the farm labourers to reverse the course of agricultural change and to return to the security of traditional morality when farmers recognised their responsibility to provide employment for their men. Therefore agricultural machinery, especially threshing machines which reduced the amount of winter employment, were a principal target for the riots. Also, poor law overseers found themselves, in some areas, the object of the crowd's attentions because of the harsh and degrading treatment of the unemployed in receipt of parish relief.

In Hampshire, Sussex, Berkshire, Wiltshire and Dorset, one prevelant form of disturbance was the assembly of bodies of men who marched from village to village destroying machinery and demanding money, food or drink, sometimes as a 'reward' for their work. Collective begging was an integral part of the proceedings and this form of charity was common to many ceremonies, such as Christmas wassailing and Mummers visits. A 'treasurer' was appointed to collect the money and to act as overseer for its distribution. This was again, common practice in ceremonial visitations. Joseph Carter was treasurer for the crowd at Barton Stacey. He told Alexander Somerville some fifteen years later that: 'they said I wor honest, and they gave it to me to carry. I had £40 at one time - £40 every shilling'.[1]

Collective begging was no new development. A food riot at Norwich in 1740 followed much the same pattern:

> Early on Thursday Morning, by sound of Horns, they met again; and after a short confabulation, divided into Parties, and march'd out of Town at different Gates, with a long streamer carried before them, purposing to visit the Gentlemen and Farmers in the neighbouring villages, in order to extort Money, Strong Ale, etc from them. At many places, where the Generosity of People answer'd not their Expectations, 'tis said they shew'd their Resentment by treading down the Corn in the fields.[2]

1 Alexander Somerville, *The whistler at the plough* (Manchester, 1852) p. 263.

2 Thompson, 'Moral economy', p. 111.

The summoning of the crowd by the blowing of cow's horns was general practice in the 1830 disturbances. However, the 'doleing riots', as this form of action might be termed, did not only utilise some elements of folk behaviour as a model. November and December were the principal months in which the upheavals occurred. They were also the months in which were clustered several Saints days when collective begging was sanctioned. The feasts of St Clement (23 November), St Catherine (25 November), St Andrew (30 November), St Nicholas (6 December) and St Thomas (21 December) all figured significantly in the customary calendar. Squirreling on St Andrew's day has already been noticed. St Catherine and St Clement were important 'doleing' days in many parts of Hampshire and Sussex when parties of the 'weaker' members of the community, women, children, widows or the aged, were permitted to solicit contributions from neighbouring farms and houses, on behalf of themselves and their families. Money and victuals collected on these visits provided the labouring poor with some measure of relief from hardship during the Christmas period. In Sussex a rhyme was chanted by the assemblies, a version of which was used in various places:

> Cattern' and Clemen' be here, here, here,
> Give us your apples and give us your beer,
> One for Peter,
> Two for Paul,
> Three for Him who made us all;
> Clemen' was a good man,
> Cattern' was his mother;
> Give us your best,
> And not your worst,
> And God will give your soul good rest.[1]

Similar folk activity took place on St Thomas's day when groups of women and children went from door to door asking for contributions of money or food and drink.[2] This was usually known as 'going a gooding' or in some places 'a mumping' or 'a corning'. The latter form involved the farmers giving small quantities of corn to their visitors.

It was not surprising that Captain Swing's operations took place at this point of 'life crisis' in the year. Charity was traditionally expected at times of most economic pressure by the labouring poor. The doleing customs provided a model for action and it is possible that members of the crowd felt that their behaviour was legitimated by reference to customary practice and to the concept of traditional moral behaviour which acted as a force for both forms of activity. They had stepped beyond the bounds of institutionalised folklore but had adapted its mechanism for use in more direct forms of behaviour. The riots were, with some exceptions, well-disciplined and restrained. Damage was confined to the destruction of machinery and no life was lost. In Dorset it was reported that:

> The mob, urged on from behind hedges, by a number of women and children, advanced rather respectfully, and with their hats in their hands, to demand increases in wages.

1 Sawyer, 'Sussex folklore', p. 252.

2 Sawyer, 'Sussex folklore', p. 253.

Some of the county gentry who had been despatched to quell the riots:

> described the mob they had encountered as being in general very fine-looking young men, and particularly well dressed, as if they had put on their best clothes for the occassion.[1]

The wearing of Sunday clothes was a feature of much customary behaviour.

The demand for contributions was a general feature of the disturbances and it was considered necessary, in the address of the Grand Jury at Winchester Assizes when the rioters were tried, to clarify the legal position regarding such levies:

> The cases of robbery from the person, likely to become the subject of our present inquiry, may be found to differ in the circumstances, but not in principle, from the ordinary attacks of robbers, familiar to all who are in the habit of frequenting our Courts of Criminal Justice. They will as far as I am able to judge from the depositions, be found to have been perpetrated by tumultous mobs, armed with offensive weapons, traversing the country, and requiring money, victuals, drink, and other articles, sometimes under the practice of alms or contributions to relieve some real or supposed grievance.[2]

The motive which impelled those who begged for charity on the 'doleing days' which occurred in November and December, also acted on some of the Swing rioters as an implicit unconscious response to life crises in the calendrical cycle. Traditional practice and open protest sprang from the same cultural experience and often intermingled or followed a similar pattern.

In some of the disturbances in Sussex, forms of ritual were noticeably present. The expulsion of poor law officials and holders of tithes either occurred or were threatened in some ten Sussex communities: Battle, Brede, Brightling, Burwash, Fairlight, Heathfield, Mayfield, Ninfield, Ticehurst and Warbleton.[3]

The well-documented events which took place at Brede where Mr Thomas Abel was Assistant Overseer and Governor of the Poor House, illustrate the extent of the ritual activity of the crowd. Some one hundred and fifty persons, including many women and children, assembled before Mr Abel's house and tried to force an entry. They brought with them the handcart used by the unemployed on parish relief to haul stones when working on the road. Their intention was to secure Abel and transport him, in the cart, to the parish limits. After some initial resistance, Abel surrendered himself to the crowd, on the promise that

1 W H Parry Okeden, 'The agricultural riots in Dorset in 1830', *Dorset Natural History and Archaeological Society*, LII (1930) 90-1.

2 *A report of the proceedings at the Special Commission holden at Winchester, December 20th 1830, and eight following days* (London, 1831) pp. 11-12.

3 Eric J Hobsbawm and George Rudé, *Captain Swing* (Lawrence & Wishart, 1969) p. 79.

he would not be harmed, and took his place in the cart. In fact, he was given the opportunity to choose where he wanted to be taken and, at his request, the crowd conveyed him to Vinehall, some six miles from the parish. The cart was pulled by women and children and a group of labourers marched alongside in mock imitation of a military bodyguard, carrying their staves over their shoulders like rifles. The whole occasion appeared to be accompanied with great festivity and Abel recounted in his deposition: 'that many of the persons wore ribbands in their hats'.[1]

A report of the incident illustrates the close similarity of the crowd's actions to the ritual associated with 'rough music':

> The villagers brought the cart to Abel's door, seized him and placed him in it with a rope round his neck, to which a large stone was tied. Without scarcely an exception, the whole of the inhabitants accompanied the labourers, who thus drew him out of the parish attended by 'rough music'. They at first fixed on the parish of Westfield to deposit their load; but his fame having extended to that hamlet, he was rejected by the people, and the procession bent their steps to Vinehall, near Robertsbridge, where it appears, rubbish-like, he was 'shot out' of the cart into the road and there left with this blessing, - that if ever he made his appearance again at Brede he would get his head broke.[2]

Joseph Bryant, one of the leaders of the crowd, described the events, emphasising the use of the parish cart as the mode of transport:

> We went back to the workhouse and the cart that Mr Abel had made for the men to draw on the Road was there and then the farmers went in and persuaded Mr Abel to come out and then he came out with them and got up into the Cart himself . . . and we carried him there (Vinehall) or drew him there in the cart the women and the men altogether.[3]

It is significant that women and children played an active role in the ritual drawing of the cart to Vinehall. Women and children were the weak elements in the normal structure of the community and, therefore, their central role was a symbolic demonstration of strength and an added humiliation in what was a form of role reversal. Mr Abel was being ritually demoted and the inferior members of the community performed the main task, thereby confirming his total degradation and emphasising their triumph.

The element of community was also central to the proceedings at Brede. In this case ritual emphasised unity between groups in the community in opposition to an outside agent. The labourers were not acting alone but were supported by many of the leading farmers, as

1 Thomas Abel's depostion, dated 6 November 1830 (PRO, HO 52/10, ff. 402-3).

2 Bernard Reaney, *The class struggle in 19th century Oxfordshire: the social and communal background to the Otmoor disturbances of 1830 to 1835* (Oxford History Workshop Pamphlets, No. 3, 1971) p. 111.

3 Deposition of Joseph Bryant concerning Mr Abel, dated 19 November 1830 (PRO, HO 52/10, f. 488).

Bryant's statement made evident:

> When we came back . . . Mr Coleman was there of Chitcomb and he gave every one of us half a pint of Beer women and men and Mr Reed of Brede High gave us a Barrel because we had done such a great thing in the Parish as to carry that man away and Mr Coleman said he never was better pleased in his life than with the day's work which had been done.[1]

Abel's expulsion was central to the unity between farmers and labourers and the commensality accompanying the proceedings was indicative of their co-operation and confirmation of the traditional pattern of relationships. It cannot be overlooked that such commensality was a common feature of many folk customs and ceremonies and that the concept of reward for due labour lay at the heart of much folk activity. It is also important that, rightly or wrongly, many of the labourers involved in machine-breaking often demanded their contribution in the form of money or victuals as a reward for their destructive work and, when such donations were forthcoming, they gave hearty thanks before the crowd moved on to the next farm. By referring to elements common to certain folk usages such as solidarity between groups in the community, expressed in commensality and exchange of service, the labourers, in the collective action of machine-breaking, wished to eliminate the stigma of illegality. At Brede, the crowd were supported in their actions by the farmers and the hospitality extended to them after Abel's removal must have acted as a strong legitimating influence. Bryant continued: 'We told the farmers when we come back that we would always assist them as far as laid in our power all of us'.[2]

Similar occurrences took place at Warbleton where a crowd gathered, 'for the purpose of compelling the assistant overseer to leave the parish against his will'. While at Ninfield the labourers were later accused of: 'forcibly removing Samuel Skinner the assistant overseer from whence they took him to Battel in a cart drawn by women and children'.[3] Here the ritual role of inferior groups in the community was again stressed.

Thus it would appear that, in some areas of Sussex, ritual was an important feature in movements of protest, stressing the elements of community solidarity and commensality often found in folk forms where the demonstration of strength against identifiable enemies to traditional moral behaviour was also a conscious feature of protest.

Popular disturbance against enclosure did not figure significantly in the Captain Swing riots, except in the neighbourhood of Otmoor in Oxfordshire where there was a long tradition of opposition to the enclosure and drainage of the moor and to the loss of rights of common.[4]

1 Deposition of Joseph Bryant.

2 Deposition of Joseph Bryant.

3 PRO, HO 52/10, f. 501.

4 A full account of the Otmoor disturbances can be found in Reaney, *Class struggle*.

The moor was enclosed and drained by Act of Parliament in 1815. Yet the spirit of resentment did not disappear. In August and September 1830 groups of men gathered to pull down fences and uproot hedges on the moor in the mistaken belief that a judgment in favour of some small farmers who had broken the river banks and flooded the moor the previous June to prevent their own land from being flooded, ruled all enclosures on the moor null and void.

Perhaps because of the continuous tradition of opposition, the events at Otmoor reflect a strong pattern of folk belief. Firstly it was believed that the land had originally been donated by an unknown lady who had decreed that the people could have, for common usage, as much land as she could ride round while an oat sheaf was burning. The name Otmoor, it was suggested, was a corruption of Oatmoor.[1] Also, there was a widely held belief that the land was the gift of Queen Elizabeth or some other Queen or of Charles I. Thus, the history of Otmoor was bound up in folk legend.[2]

Many of the nightly depredations were accompanied by recognisable folk forms. It was reported that 'large bodies of men in disguises' committed 'acts of outrage' on the moor. These visits occurred almost every night from 28 August to 6 September 1830. Other accounts confirmed that some of the men blackened their faces and others were in disguise.[3] On the night of 31 August the depredations increased in number and many:

> came in disguise with their faces blackened, and some with partly women's clothes. They began cutting some trees of about ten year's growth on the Oddington side of the moor, . . . Whenever a tree fell, a shout of exultation was raised with a blowing of horns, heard at the distance of two or three miles.[4]

The summoning of the rioters by blowing horns and their continued use during their operations was common in the Otmoor disturbances. The wearing of female attire was favoured by several members of the crowd. Such ritual forms, which can be found in much folk activity, were significant to the rioters in their demonstration of strength and solidarity. They were reopening the moor and restoring traditional patterns of communal life and, for this reason, their intentions were made clear to the proprietors of Otmoor through ritual action.

6 September was the day when Otmoor was formally re-possessed by the neighbouring communities. The model used for this action was clearly the annual parish perambulation, when the boundaries of the

1 Reaney, *Class struggle*, p. 12.

2 PRO, HO 52/9: The account to the Home Office of Rev. Theophilus Cooke dated 13 September 1830. 'They had . . . an old prejudice that Otmoor belonged to the poor of the Otmoor towns, and had been given them by Queen Elizabeth, . . . this is totally void of foundation and the moor is precisely upon the same footing with other commons'.

3 Cooke's account, PRO, HO 52/9.

4 Cooke's account, PRO, HO 52/9.

parish were ceremonially reaffirmed by a procession of officials and members of the community. These 'ganging' days, as they were sometimes known, usually took place in Rogation Week and served the purpose of confirming parish boundaries and removing encroachments upon common or waste ground. For the labouring poor, perambulations were important because they represented the corporate action of the whole community, dispensing justice against commons infringements, defending the traditional geographic basis of the village and making a public avowal of the rights of the community to the common land. In fact, the very term 'processioning' which was used to describe this action became corrupted in the popular tongue to 'possessioning'. One such procession was observed in 1818 at a small village in Derbyshire:

> The constable and a crowd of boys constituted the procession, if such an irregular company could be so called. An axe, a mattock, and an iron crow were carried by the labourers, for the purpose of demolishing any building or fence, which had been raised without permission on the 'waste ground'.[1]

The crowd at Otmoor followed the same pattern. They decided they would:

> perambulate the whole circumsphere of Otmoor, in the manner which they state it was customary for them in former times to do, and that abandoning their nocturnal sallies they would in open daylight go possessioning and demolishing every fence which obstructed their course.[2]

In their progress round the moor, they destroyed fences, hedges and every obstacle in their path, in a thorough and systematic way. The cry of 'Otmoor for ever' was all they would say in reply to questioning by the sheriff and the yeomanry. About 1000 people took part and one farmer, who witnessed the procession noted:

> the zeal and perseverance of the women and children as well as the men, and the ease and composure with which they waded through depths of mud and water and overcame every obstacle in the march.

The same observer said that:

> he did not hear any threatening expressions against any person or his property, and he does not believe any individuals present entertained any feeling or wish beyond the assertion of what they conceived (whether correctly or erroneously) to be their prescriptive and inalienable right.[3]

A remarkable feature of the 'possessioning' of Otmoor was the use of custom and ritual borrowed from other traditional forms. The inhabitants of Great Wishford also utilised some traditional practices

1 Chambers, *Books of days*, I, 582-4.

2 Reaney, *Class struggle*, pp. 34-5.

3 *Oxford University and City Herald*, 11 September 1830, cited in John L Hammond and Lucy Barbara Hammond, *The village labourer, 1760-1832: a study in the government of England before the Reform Bill* (Longmans, 1911) p. 95.

to defend the communal right to dead wood from Grovely Forest. Folk custom was clearly potent in legitimating the actions of the crowd.

The action of the crowd at Great Wishford should be seen in a similar light to the 'possessioning' behaviour of the Otmoor disturbances. Ritual forms were adopted in both spheres of action. However, the term folklore does not adequately categorise the behaviour of wood gatherers at Great Wishford; nor does a simple attempt to describe the activities of the crowd at Otmoor as social protest, convey the complexity of ritual form present. Perhaps they are connected by being rooted in the same traditional culture of the eighteenth-century rural community. The use of ceremony was consistant. At certain times of the year when deprivation was imminent or in response to transgressors of traditional community behaviour, the labouring poor resorted to the same identifiable and constant patterns of ritual or customary activity. It can be seen that elements of social conflict lay behind much folk practice and that folk ritual occurred, in some instances, in more orthodox movements of protest.

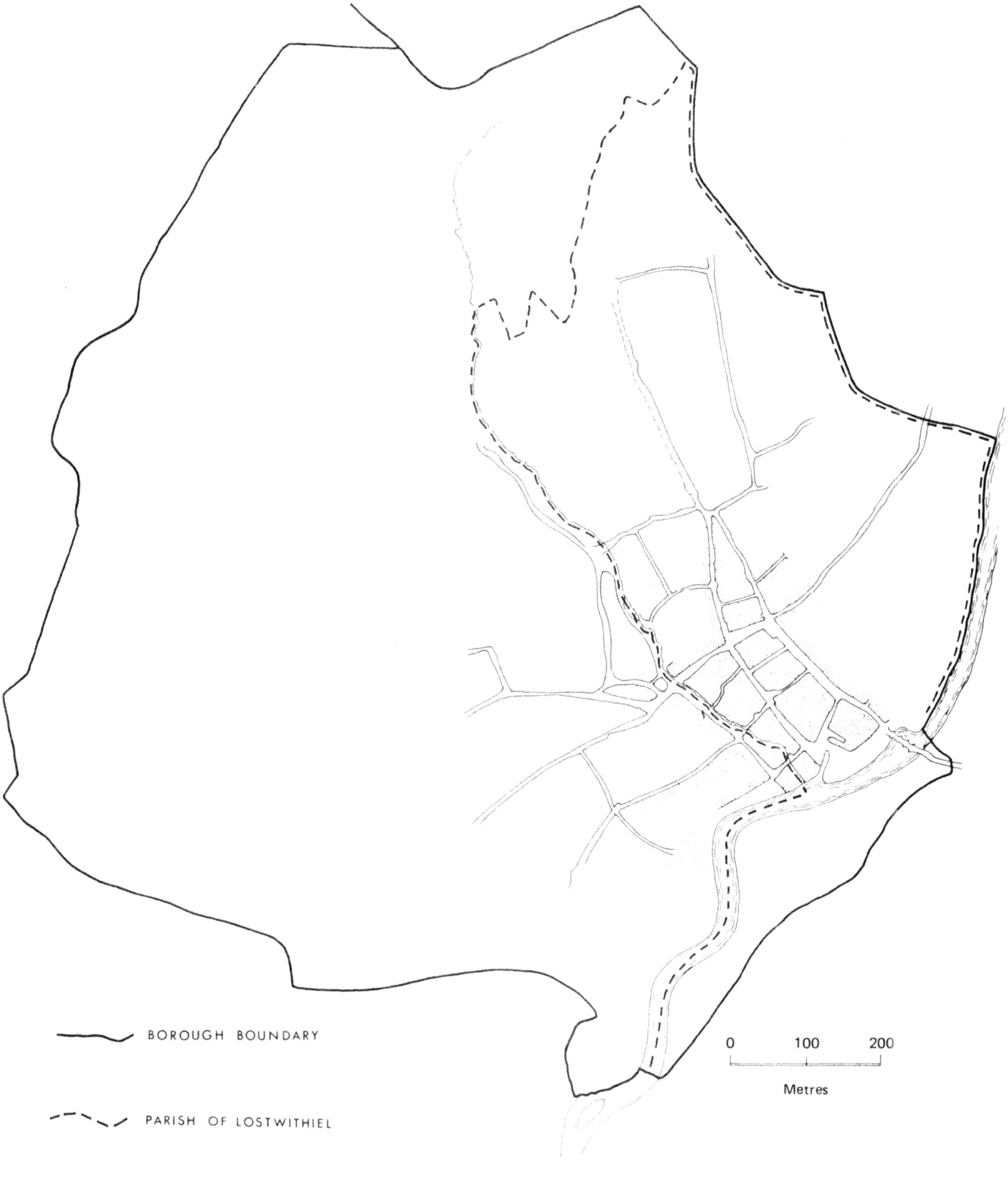

FIGURE 1

The borough of Lostwithiel and the Lostwithiel-Lanlivery parish boundary

THE SOCIAL STRUCTURE OF LOSTWITHIEL IN THE EARLY NINETEENTH CENTURY

Norman J G Pounds

The borough of Lostwithiel was created in the twelfth century. The oldest surviving charter, granted by Robert de Cardinham, belongs to the 1190s, though the small town may have originated even earlier. It lay on the right bank of the River Fowey, 6 miles from the sea and near the limit of navigation. It was a planned town, consisting of three east to west streets, lying roughly parallel to one another, and intersected by several north-south streets. Lostwithiel is the only clear example in south-western England of a medieval planned town. It reached to within a few yards of the river on the east and on the south was bounded by a brook, the Cob or Cober, which drove the town mill before emptying into the Fowey. South of the Cob, and thus outside the limits of the early borough, another settlement with a vaguely urban character grew up. It was no doubt sponsored by the lord of the manor of Bodardle in which it lay and its inhabitants probably hoped to share in the prosperity of Lostwithiel. This satellite was the borough of Penkneth or Penknight.

In the middle years of the thirteenth century a Cardinham heiress conveyed her rights over Lostwithiel as well as the nearby manor and castle of Restormel to Richard, Earl of Cornwall and King of the Romans. Soon afterwards Earl Richard acquired the manor of Penknight, which derived from the manor of Bodardle, together with its rights over Lostwithiel's diminutive neighbour, the borough of Penknight. In 1268 Earl Richard granted a charter to the borough of Lostwithiel and Penknight.[1] The two were in process of merging to form a single borough which in time came to be known only as Lostwithiel. Penknight disappeared as a separate borough but the social and institutional consequences of this early division lasted until late in the nineteenth century and the two boroughs continue to be readily distinguishable in the landscape. For Penknight was not a planned or planted borough. It grew as an irregular cluster of huts close to the south bank of the Cob brook and such it has remained.[2]

At a relatively early date in its history Lostwithiel acquired a church, dedicated to St Bartholomew. It was a chapelry within the large parish of Lanlivery and it served only the original borough of Lostwithiel. The Penknight settlement remained subject to the parish church of Lanlivery which lay on the high ground a mile to the west. In the sixteenth century the chapelry became parochial but its limits were unchanged. It was the parish of the original Lostwithiel as it was before Earl Richard's charter and excluded the cluster of houses beyond the Cob brook. The spiritual needs of these were served, if indeed they were served at all, from Lanlivery.

1 'The records of the Corporation of Lostwithiel', *Historical Manuscripts Commission, Report on manuscripts in various collections*, I, 1901, 327-8.

2 Maurice W Beresford, *New towns of the middle ages: town plantation in England, Wales and Gascony* (Lutterworth Press, 1967) pp. 406-8.

The division marked by the Cob, now buried from sight in a covered culvert, did more than separate two ecclesiastical jurisdictions. It became a social barrier. The élite of Lostwithiel tended from the middle ages to the nineteenth century to live north of the Cob and it was they who ruled the borough and discriminated in favour of the sector in which they lived. Charities and endowments bequeathed to the borough as a whole came to be attached to the parish of Lostwithiel and were thus administered exclusively for the benefit of that part which lay north of the Cob. It was, however, in the administration of the Poor Law that the abuses of this system were most apparent. The poor of Lostwithiel were cared for, however inadequately, by a fairly well-to-do citizenry; those of its Penknight suburb were neglected by the distant overseers of a poor and rural parish. Not until the end of the nineteenth century was the system of local government changed and the whole borough brought in all respects under a common authority.

Lostwithiel was for its size a wealthy borough. Its landed endowments were considerable and allowed it to dispense with a church rate and until 1777 it had no need even to levy a poor rate. The lands and charities were administered by the borough in the interests of the parish of Lostwithiel. The borough supported the church and held itself responsible for its care and maintenance. It paid to keep the church clock, which for most citizens was the only timepiece, in good order and bought the sacramental bread and wine. On the other hand, such small sums as the church earned - for burials within its walls or the sale of the churchyard elms - were pocketed by the borough. Periodically the churchwardens submitted a statement of their expenses on church and parish to the mayor, which was honoured and duly recorded in the borough accounts. The citizens who lived in the Penknight suburb enjoyed none of these benefits. They paid their rates, both church and poor, to the parish of Lanlivery, though one may question whether they made the journey to the churchtown except on the rarest occasions. The citizens who lived in Lanlivery Urban, as this sector of the borough came to be called in the later nineteenth century, were thus the underprivileged members of Lostwithiel society.[1]

Population structure

Population statistics were recorded in the nineteenth century on a parochial basis. Although the majority of citizens were enumerated as parishioners of Lostwithiel parish, those who lived south of Cob brook were lost amid the total for Lanlivery. It is not possible to estimate their number before the census takers' books first became available in 1841.

The return made to Bishop Clagett's Articles in 1744 noted a total of 142 families in Lostwithiel *parish*.[2] In 1672 the Compton 'census' had recorded 300 confirmed parishioners and six nonconformists.

1 This paper is based almost entirely on the borough archives (Cornwall Record Office (CRO) B/Los/1 to 5) and the parochial documents, kept in a chest in the parish church until 1976 and now in the County Record Office as CRO, DDP/128. Individual items in these two large collections are not cited separately.

2 Copy in Henderson Calendar XI, Royal Institution of Cornwall, Truro.

These figures suggest a total population not too far from 600. The first census of 1801 gave a total of 743 but already the population had almost certainly begun to increase. By 1811 it was 825 and by 1831 had reached 1074. Until this date the census was taken by the parish overseers and their method of payment was calculated to ensure that no one was omitted. In any case, they must have had an intimate knowledge of the social structure of their parish. From 1841 the count was taken by registration officers who were required to record in printed books the name, sex, age, residence and occupation of each parishioner. In addition they were required to note whether each resident was born within or outside the county.[1] For the first time it became possible to count the population of Lanlivery Urban:

Table 1

	Households	Persons	Average household size	Percentage of borough
Lostwithiel parish	220	1186	5.4	71.5
Lanlivery Urban	103	473	4.6	28.5
	323	1659	5.1	100.0

If the ratio of the two parts of the borough to one another was similar forty years earlier, their combined population at the time of the first census would have been about 1040.

Women outnumbered men only marginally in Lanlivery Urban but overwhelmingly in Lostwithiel parish. The sex ratio (the ratio of women to men) in the borough as a whole was 113.2 but 118.8 in the parish of Lostwithiel. The reason for this disparity is not far to seek. Female domestic servants who lived in the homes of their employers were particularly numerous in Lostwithiel parish, where there were no fewer than 57, but few in Lanlivery Urban. Indeed, it is very probable that many who served in Lostwithiel were themselves the daughters of humbler citizens who lived beyond Cob brook. Without this army of domestic servants, the sex ratio of Lostwithiel would not have been remarkable.

East of Lostwithiel, on the opposite bank of the river Fowey, lay the village of Bridgend. It had formed a separate manor belonging to the Lower family and it belonged, as it still does, to the parish of St Winnow. In 1841 it was a community of 39 households and 184 inhabitants. They were almost without exception working-class people amongst whom agricultural labourers predominated. Nevertheless, there is good reason to regard Bridgend as functionally as well as geographically a part of the Lostwithiel urban settlement, even though the river Fowey formed an administrative boundary which cut far deeper than that which separated Lostwithiel parish from Lanlivery. The whole Lostwithiel-Bridgend settlement thus had a population of about 1850 in 1841. At the beginning of the century it could not have been much less than 1200.

1 Microfilm of the census takers' books, in the Public Record Office, London, for 1841 and 1851 are at the County Record Office, Truro.

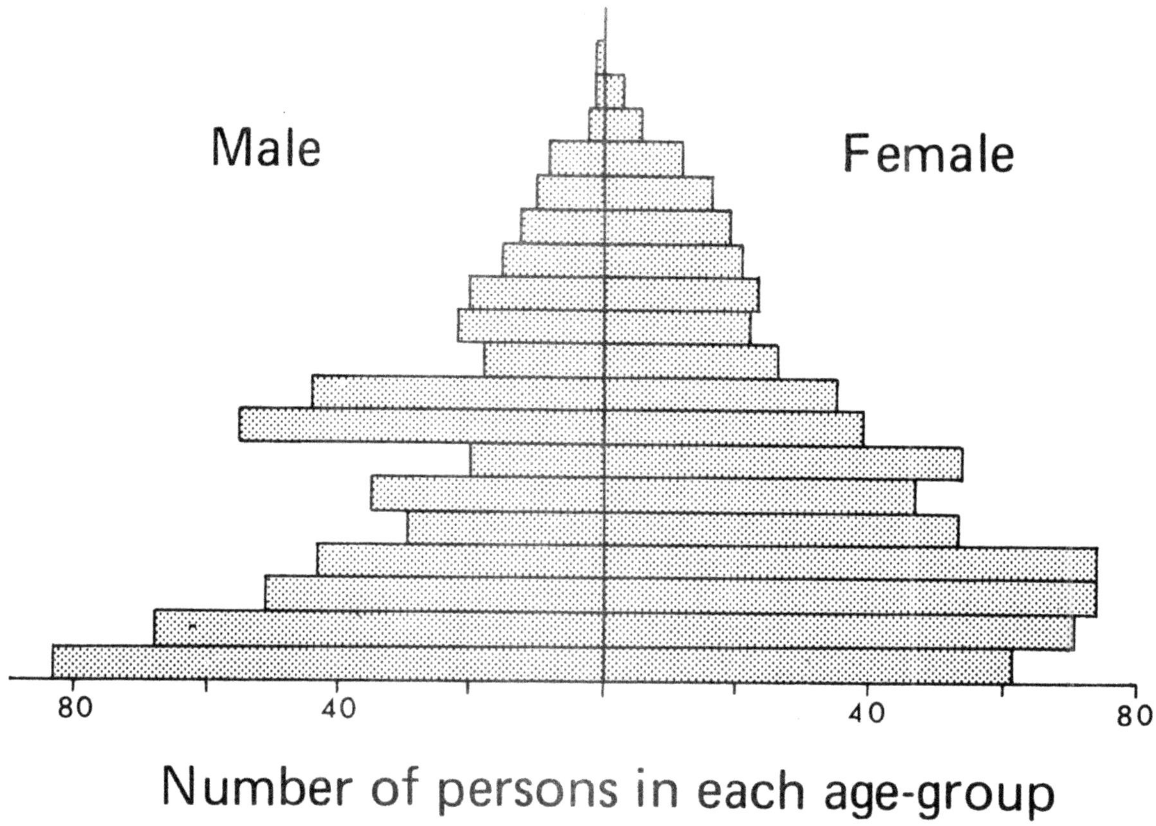

FIGURE 2

Age and sex structure of the population of the borough of Lostwithiel : based on the census of 1851

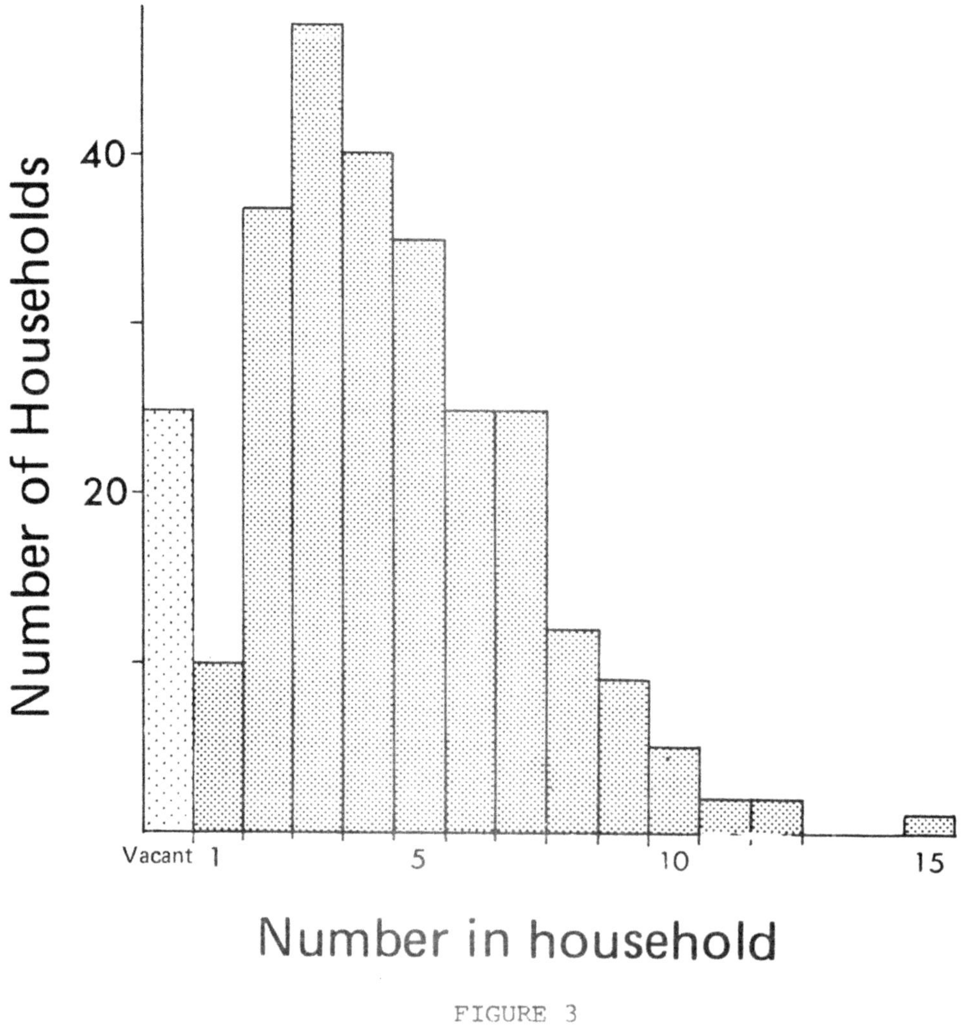

FIGURE 3

Number and size of households : based on the census of 1841

Although the census takers in 1841 were required to note the age of each inhabitant, the resulting data are far from trustworthy. Too many people appear to have rounded their ages to the nearest multiple of ten and in many cases the ages given in 1851 do not harmonise with those of 1841. The 1851 census appears in this respect to be far more reliable and it has been used in preparing the population pyramid shown in Figure 2. It is a highly irregular pyramid. It has the broad base which one would expect in a population which still had high birth-rates and death-rates. Less understandable is the inequality of the sexes. From the age of about ten to the thirties there is a marked overplus of women - almost 2 to 1. Thereafter there is an approximate equality until the expected numerical superiority of women shows itself above about 55. The inequalities in the lower age groups can be partially explained by the employment within the borough of female servants but there must also have been an out-migration of young men seeking employment in the mines, in Plymouth and even farther afield.

In 1841 there were 323 households within the borough of Lostwithiel, 220 of them in Lostwithiel parish. They ranged from single person households, of which there were seven, to complex households with extended families, lodgers and servants. Nuclear households, consisting only of parents and children, however, predominated. They made up two-thirds of the total. The 1841 census does not, however, specify the relationship between members of a household and one can only suggest on the basis of names and ages that some were grandparents and grandchildren. This was remedied in the 1851 census which enquired the relationship of each member to the head of the household. Children, parents, brothers and sisters of the householder, as well as lodgers, visitors and servants, are thus listed. Out of 313 households in 1851, no less than 58 contained relatives outside the nuclear group. These were most often grandparents and grandchildren but in a few instances a brother or sister of the head of household is named.

The average household size in 1841 was 5.14; higher - 5.4 persons - in Lostwithiel parish but lower - 4.6 - in Lanlivery Urban, a discrepancy partly accountable, as we have seen, by the greater number of domestic servants in Lostwithiel parish. It is evident also from the rate books that the actual houses were themselves smaller on average in Lanlivery Urban than in Lostwithiel parish; extended families were in consequence fewer and lodging houses less numerous. All the inns within the borough, for example, lay in Lostwithiel parish.

As a general rule, the small, working-class houses such as those of King Street, Summer Lane and of the small courts which opened off North Street, each contained only a nuclear family. In King Street, for example, only four houses out of 22 contained more than parents and children. There was, both in 1841 and 1851, a small number of large, well-appointed households, such as that of the Hexts in North Street, with butler, cook, footman and two maids, and the Foster household in Fore Street with its five servants. In addition to a couple of inns there was a number of lodging houses. These must have been miserably crowded. One mean house in King Street contained in 1841, in addition to husband and wife, five lodgers - two agricultural labourers, a miner, an ostler and a woman of no disclosed occupation. At the same time a house in Fore Street, occupied by a victualler and his wife, contained, in addition to a servant and an elderly woman, no less than twelve lodgers, all except one described as hawkers. The greater detail given by the 1851 census allows the number of such lodgers, together with their age and occupation, to be determined. There were 54, of whom no less than ten lived in a single house in Fore Street. It was run by a man described as a 'lodging house keeper and hatter' and amongst his tenants were a railway worker and a shoemaker. A few lodgers some were clearly itinerant. Most of those who let rooms to lodgers were the humblest workers, labourers or journeymen who happened to have a spare room. Many lodgers must have lived in conditions of extreme overcrowding, even of squalor. The worst case was probably that of a brushmaker and his wife whose house in Bodmin Hill contained also seven other married couples with altogether, seven children, an elderly widower and a maidservant, in all 25 persons. The house in question has not yet been identified but, given the character of the houses in Bodmin Hill, there cannot have been less than five persons to a room. It is not surprising that the borough council began the inspection and licensing of lodging houses.

The society of Lostwithiel was far from static. In 1841 almost 80 residents of the borough had been born outside the county. It was not until 1851 that the parish of birth was recorded. The data collected demonstrate how mobile the population was. Most children had been born in the borough but occasionally the elder children had been born elsewhere, thus showing when the family moved to Lostwithiel. If, however, one takes only parents and heads of households, one finds that only 29.5 per cent of the men and 21.5 per cent of the women had actually been born in the borough. More than 10 per cent had been born outside the county and 60 per cent of the men and nearly 70 per cent of the women had migrated to the borough from elsewhere in the county. Most had come only a short distance, no more than ten miles. Few had come from the north-east and east of the county, where the counter-attraction of Plymouth was probably too great, and many of those from west of Truro were miners attracted to Fowey Consols or Restormel Iron Mine.

People were less mobile in the early years of the century than they were in the 1840s. Nevertheless the parish registers at intervals record unfamiliar names as new families moved into the borough. The degree of mobility is best seen in the depositions made before the magistrates by those who had become chargeable to the rates. They give the impression that many of the young were apprenticed outside the borough; that some absconded and that most moved from one short term job to another until destitution forced them to turn to the parish overseers for help. This mobility was most apparent amongst the humblest members of Lostwithiel society. No doubt the sons of the prosperous tradesmen and craftsmen worked in their family businesses until the time came to inherit them. Such people were rarely if ever called upon to make depositions before the borough magistrates.

Structure of employment

In 1841 the census gave the occupations of 437 persons in addition to 38 who were described as 'independent'. More than 40 per cent of all employed persons were engaged in a craft and about half as many in agriculture. Over fifty were merchants or retailers, including 14 hawkers, and 27 were professional men, teachers, agents or clerks.

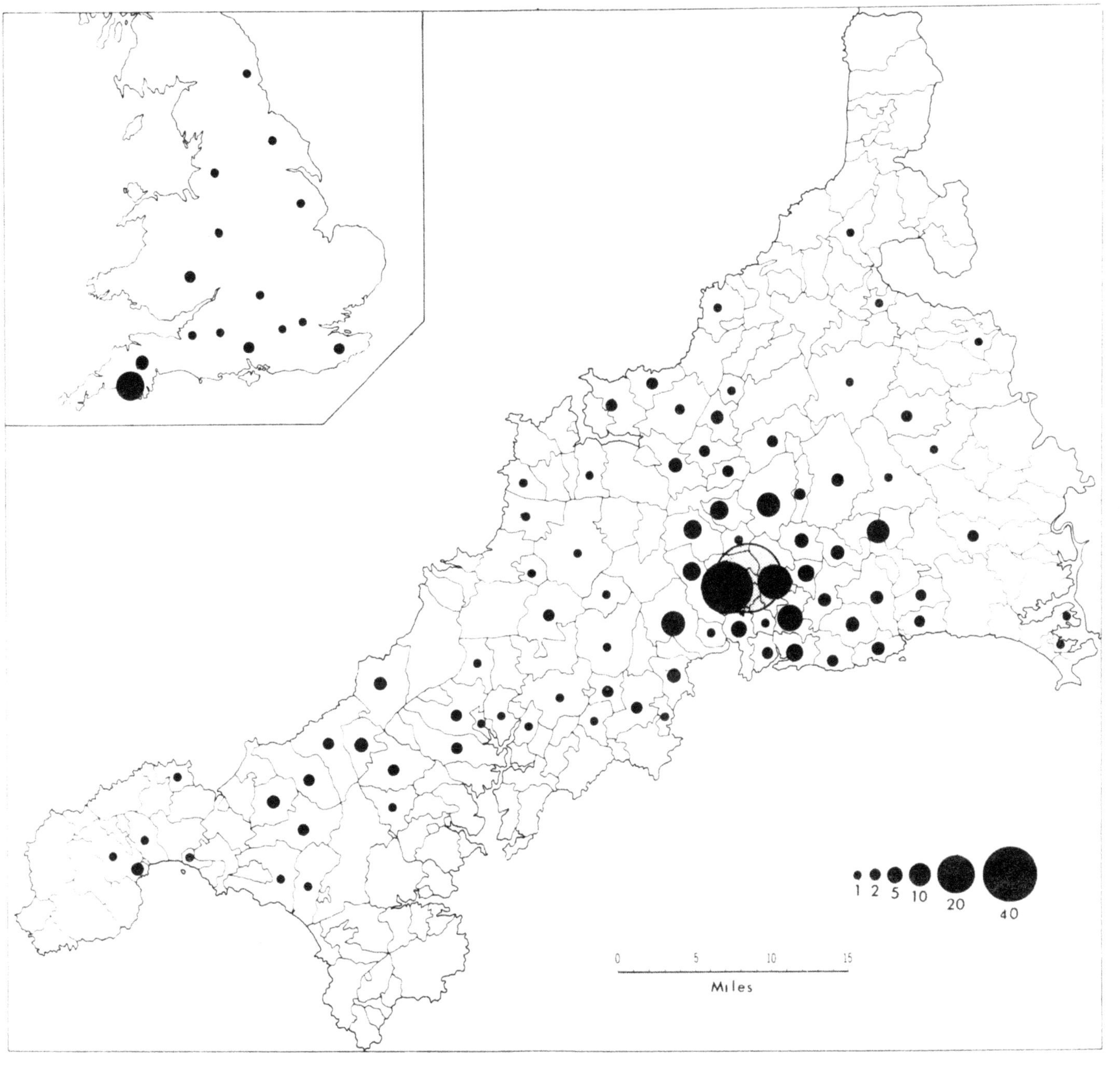

FIGURE 4

Birthplaces of the population of Lostwithiel : based on the census of 1851

Table 2

Craftsmen:	Leather working (including 29 shoemakers)	41	
	Clothing (including 17 tailors)	31	
	Building (including 21 masons)	30	
	Woodworking (including 19 carpenters, 13 cabinet makers)	44	
	Metal-working (including 11 blacksmiths)	15	
	Others (including 15 woolcombers)	26	
			187
Miners			54
Agricultural workers (including 81 agricultural labourers)			93
Semi-skilled and unskilled workers (including 14 watermen)			25
Merchants, retailers, shopkeepers (including 14 hawkers)			51
Professional people, teachers, clerks			27
			437

This total excludes the population of Bridgend which was predominantly rural in its pursuits. There were no tanners or leather workers; very few tailors, masons or other craftsmen, and retailers were limited to two butchers and a grocer. On the other hand, there were seven basket makers, a craft not met with in the borough. More than 40 per cent of the employed population was made up of farmers or agricultural labourers. Bridgend, despite its nearness to Lostwithiel, was in most respects a village and its inhabitants must have relied on the shops and services of Lostwithiel.

The 437 who were economically active in the borough of Lostwithiel made goods and performed services for themselves and for a population living within a relatively small radius. Within 10 miles lay the towns of Liskeard, Bodmin, Fowey and St Austell, each of them larger and with a greater range of economic activity than Lostwithiel itself. The service area of the town was a small one. Many of those listed in the census served only the local community: the six teachers, the chimney sweep, the two washerwomen, the religious ministers and the medical men. It is doubtful whether those employed in the building industry travelled far afield for work and dressmakers and tailors, milliners and hatters must also have found their customers largely in the local community. Other workers must have provided goods and services for the surrounding rural population; 29 shoemakers were more than enough for a community of less than 1700 and 13 cabinet makers, 5 millwrights and 4 coopers would have been gravely underemployed without customers from outside the borough. These, together with the miners who were mostly employed at the Restormel Iron Mine, and the surveyors, mine agents and excise officer brought money into the borough, as also did the 38 persons of independent means. The activities of these groups were basic to the community; without them there could have been no monetary inflow; no way of acquiring necessary goods and services which were not generated within.

The community of Lostwithiel as late as the mid-nineteenth century still lived close to the land. Very many of the craftsmen and shop-keepers also leased or owned smallholdings or even farms in the close proximity of the town. This is shown in the Tithe Apportionments of neighbouring parishes. The Corporation itself owned about 140 acres together with several houses, spread over Lostwithiel, Lanlivery and St Winnow parishes, which it generally leased on lives to its own burgesses. Few houses within the borough were without some kind of garden or orchard and most of the population was able to satisfy at least in part its need for garden produce. Many houses had stables and the manure heap before the front door was far from uncommon. Some residents also kept pigs in the small enclosures behind their houses and it was not until late in the nineteenth century, as the minutes of the borough council show, that people became too sensitive to stand the nuisances which resulted. The agricultural labourers - 81 in number - must have been employed in the fields around the town, contributing very materially to its food supply.

Social structure

The community of Lostwithiel formed a spectrum from the very poor to the relatively well-to-do. The latter were few in number and most of those who owned property within the borough and were closely associated with its affairs, lived in fact beyond its limits. Foremost among them were the Edgcumbes, the Kendalls and the Hexts. The Edgcumbes lived in the far south-east of the county, looking across the Hamoaze to Plymouth, but maintained a town house in Lostwithiel, a severe granite building in Fore Street, which today houses the local government offices. The Hexts lived at Restormel House, below the castle ruins to the north of the town, but some members of the family resided in the handsome house which is today no. 23 North Street. The Kendalls lived at Pelyn, in Lanlivery, and maintained a town house in Bodmin Hill. Others among the gentry, like the Rashleighs and Gregors, had links with the borough and served as capital burgesses but took little part in the day to day running of its affairs.

At the opposite end of the social scale were the poor and destitute. We know a great deal about those who were in some degree supported by the borough or parish because nothing was spent on them without close scrutiny of their needs. The number receiving relief varied from less than ten to twenty or more. Most received outdoor relief, a shilling or two a week and usually clothing and other necessities. They appear most often to have lodged in the town, frequently with relatives. There was however a poor house, which had been established in the 1770s. It lay close to the house of the wealthy local tanner, Richard Foster, who in 1798 offered to buy it and to give the borough another site for its poor house, situated at a greater distance from his residence. In the end a new poor house was created out of a house and garden near the Parade. The poor house - both the old and the new - was a converted cottage. Conditions were austere. The rooms were sparsely furnished and the beds of straw or chaff, quantities of which were periodically purchased for this purpose by the overseers. Small sums were spent at frequent intervals on minor repairs to the poor house, its chimneys, glazing and above all its 'bog-house' which must have constituted a public nuisance of major proportions. No wonder Richard Foster wanted to have it removed as far as possible from his home.

During the eighteenth century most of the poor were elderly and infirm. Those lodged in the poor house seem in general to have lacked other forms of accommodation and to have been able to look after themselves. Occasionally a woman, widowed or deserted, was placed here with her brood of children. Joseph Pawley, a violent lunatic, was given a room and restrained by a chain made by a local blacksmith. Occupants of the poor house were as a general rule long-term residents who remained here until they died and received a pauper's funeral at the expense of the parish. Their clothes were provided by the overseers and made by local tailors and seamstresses for whom the poor law business must have provided a useful supplement. Their bills, scribbled on small scraps of paper, have survived in their hundreds. Occasionally a sum was paid for washing one of the poor house inmates or for cleansing his or her clothes. The amount was large, often a shilling or more with sometimes a quantity of brandy, showing how distasteful the task must have been.

Outdoor relief was provided for those who had a room in which to live and dependants to watch over them. Less is known of their intimate needs but they collected their weekly allowance, authorised by the borough council and paid by the overseers, and at intervals were allowed a new article of clothing, not without some discussion about whether it was really necessary and an assurance that it was suited to their station.

Although much is known about the destitute, little can be said of those who hovered on the brink of destitution. Occasionally sickness or a broken limb pushed them into dependence on the parish and for a few weeks they were the recipients of parish charity. The children of paupers were viewed as little more than a nuisance. Their mothers or guardians received the small sum of sixpence a week to support them. A few - how they were chosen is not apparent - were given some schooling and all were apprenticed at the earliest age possible. There was a reluctance to take parish apprentices and at times it became necessary to ballot for them amongst potential employers. Even so the latter were commonly paid as much as £4 for the indentures of a parish apprentice. The girls were usually apprenticed to the euphemistically named craft of housewifery; in other words, they became domestic drudges. Boys were sometimes taught a useful trade but many were apprenticed to masters who could have had nothing to teach them and grew up to be unskilled labourers.

The concept of unemployment was foreign to the thinking of most people at this time. If people were unable to support themselves this could only have been because, through youth or old age, illness or accident, they were unable to do so. Such persons were to be supported but only at such a minimal level of subsistence that they would return to work as speedily as they could. Most occupations, however, called for tools and a stock of materials and the overseers not infrequently obtained such small items as would allow a pauper to make his or her way without further help from the ratepayer. A spinning turn, a pair of cards for carding wool, gates for a loom and a pit saw were thus acquired for indigent members of the community. In 1820 'a new spade [was] purchased for John Vane' but was to remain 'the property of the parish until he has paid for it'. At about the same time Nancy Leavers applied for an oven and a stock of flour and fuel 'to commence the penny-pie business'. This praiseworthy entrepreneur was, however, disappointed, because 'many of the payers of poor rates being themselves in the same line it was thought that an injury could be done to them by granting it'. Polly Netherton was more fortunate. She requested 'a new Pack-saddle for her Neddy' and got it. She was evidently an entrepreneur in the field of local transport. William Netherton, probably her brother, applied successfully for 'a pair of wheels for his cart'. Rose Lucas was allowed 2s 6d a week while learning 'the business of a mantilla maker'. This craft does not again appear in the borough records so that it is unlikely that Rose made a living in this way. Occasionally the overseers allowed money to a man to buy a stock of the raw material on which he usually worked; James Brown was thus given 10s to buy wood for making 'spear rods'.

The level of unemployment after the Napoleonic Wars was quite beyond the power of the Lostwithiel Vestry either to comprehend or to cope with. After 1816 an increasing number of men applied for relief because remunerative work was not available and the Vestry with some reluctance authorised payments of 2s or 3s a week to many of them. Some were refused help as long as they had personal effects which could be sold and the overseers were ordered 'to make some abatement in the temporary relief which has been advanced to many poor persons'.

The Vestry resorted to two devices to create employment and thus to take people off the rates. The first was a variant of the roundsman system, by which the unemployed were offered work in turn by the wealthier ratepayers of the parish at less than the prevailing rate and were given a small supplementary payment by the overseers.[1] The scheme proved inoperable; too many parishioners refused when their turn came to provide work for the unemployed and in December 1816, the Vestry resolved that the unemployed 'be paid *[wholly]* by the parish and sent to the inhabitants for employment'. It mattered little perhaps how the system was administered; those who paid the heavier poor rates received the benefit of subsidised labour.

The second device, which appears to have replaced the ineffective roundsman system, was to create work within the parish. From 1819 to 1822 and again from 1825 to 1829 the overseers worked the town quarry on Terrace Hill. The unemployed were engaged at minimum rates to quarry stone. In February 1821 some of them asked for an increase in pay and were given an additional penny a day. Two months later wages were reduced to 1s 3d a day and additional men were taken on at only 1s a day. A daily wage was later replaced by a system of payment by piecework, the men receiving 1s 6d a load and providing their own tools. The cost of tools and gunpowder, the frequent charges for 'sharping' and 'steeling' (ie tempering) the gads, picks and 'boryers', in addition to the wages, low as they were, of the unskilled quarrymen, ensured that this would be a losing venture. The overseers had difficulty in disposing of the stone. Inevitably employment in the quarry was highest and the output of stone greatest at times when unemployment was most acute and the local economy most depressed. In the end the venture was abandoned. In six years £97 had been spent and the income from the sale of stone amounted only to £53 6s 1½d. Against the loss of some £45, the Vestry could at least set the saving through the non-payment of relief to the quarry workers.

Another form of relief to the poor was the sale to them of corn at reduced prices. In 1800-1 the sum of 18s 11d was advanced to the poor to enable them to buy corn and in 1801-2 the overseers recorded the receipt of £1 10s 7½d for barley and flour sold to the poor. The most ambitious scheme for subsidising food was implemented in 1812, a year of great scarcity and high prices. The harvest in 1811 had been poor and little corn was brought to market during the following year. Distress increased in late spring and early summer as stocks were

1 Sydney G and Edith O A Checkland, ed. *The Poor Law Report of 1834* (Harmondsworth: Penguin Books, 1974) pp. 102-6.

exhausted. At this juncture Thomas Hext made an interest-free loan of £140 to the overseers for the purchase of barley for resale to the poor of the parish. A hundred bushels were thus acquired together with a further 20 bushels 12 gallons, Liskeard measure, bought from the barton of Cartuther, near Liskeard. The corn was distributed at weekly sales, beginning on 1 May. By the sixteenth week (14 August) the whole amount had been sold 'and the new corn is becoming plentiful and a drop has taken place in the price of it'.

Altogether, allowing for wastage, about 123 bushels of barley were sold. A record was kept of sales and of the names of those who bought it, together with the size of their families. No single family purchased corn every week and few bought on more than five or six occasions. The sales were managed by the overseers and justices and in all 70 families, with a total population of about 350 - about a quarter of the borough's population - purchased corn in this way. The list included some who were on poor relief but the great majority was made up of humble craftsmen and shopkeepers. By mid-July scarcity was acute in rural parishes as well as in the borough and 'we were obliged', wrote the compiler of the record, 'to limit the supply to two thirds of the demand'. By the end of the twelfth week 225 persons had benefitted, 'the greatest part of which must have remained without bread had they not been supplied by this depôt'. When the sale of corn had been completed it was found that in all £164 1s had been spent in obtaining it and that it had been sold for £137 1s. The deficit of £27 was borne by the poor rate. As they closed their books on this enterprise, the justices and overseers, in self-congratulatory mood, noted that 'there has seldom so much good been done by the sacrifice of so small a sum of money'.

The affluent members of Lostwithiel society made up no more than 1 or 2 per cent of the population. At any one time the destitute may have made up a somewhat greater proportion but it is impossible to know how many hovered on the brink of destitution, at the mercy of illness, accident or unemployment. A check of the names of those applying for relief suggests that a tenth of the population lived at or below the poverty line. A few were drunkards and ne'er-do-wells; some were widows with small children, but apart from the aged and the sick, most were unskilled workers, men who had never completed an apprenticeship or learned a craft and who, as their depositions before the magistrates show, had drifted from one job to another until they had run out of work and called upon the parish for support.

Between the extremes of rich and very poor was the broad mass of Lostwithiel citizens, at least 80 per cent of the total, who paid the poor rate and ran the borough's affairs. The only measure which survives of their wealth and social standing is the rateable value of their houses. The earliest surviving rate books, however, do not always distinguish between the value of the house and that of gardens, orchards and other properties held by the proprietor. Nevertheless, the rate on a single house in Lostwithiel parish ranged in 1803-5 from as little as 6d to 12s for the house and garden of the Rev. Jonathan Clapp; of Major Fortescue, and the Rev. Mr Kendall or the Earl of Mount Edgcumbe's town house. The range in style of housing and also in the level of wealth to support it was evidently very great. The average rate on those houses for which the data can be isolated was about 4s 6d. Unfortunately the addresses of the ratepayers are given in only a few instances. It is evident, however, from a comparison of the rate books

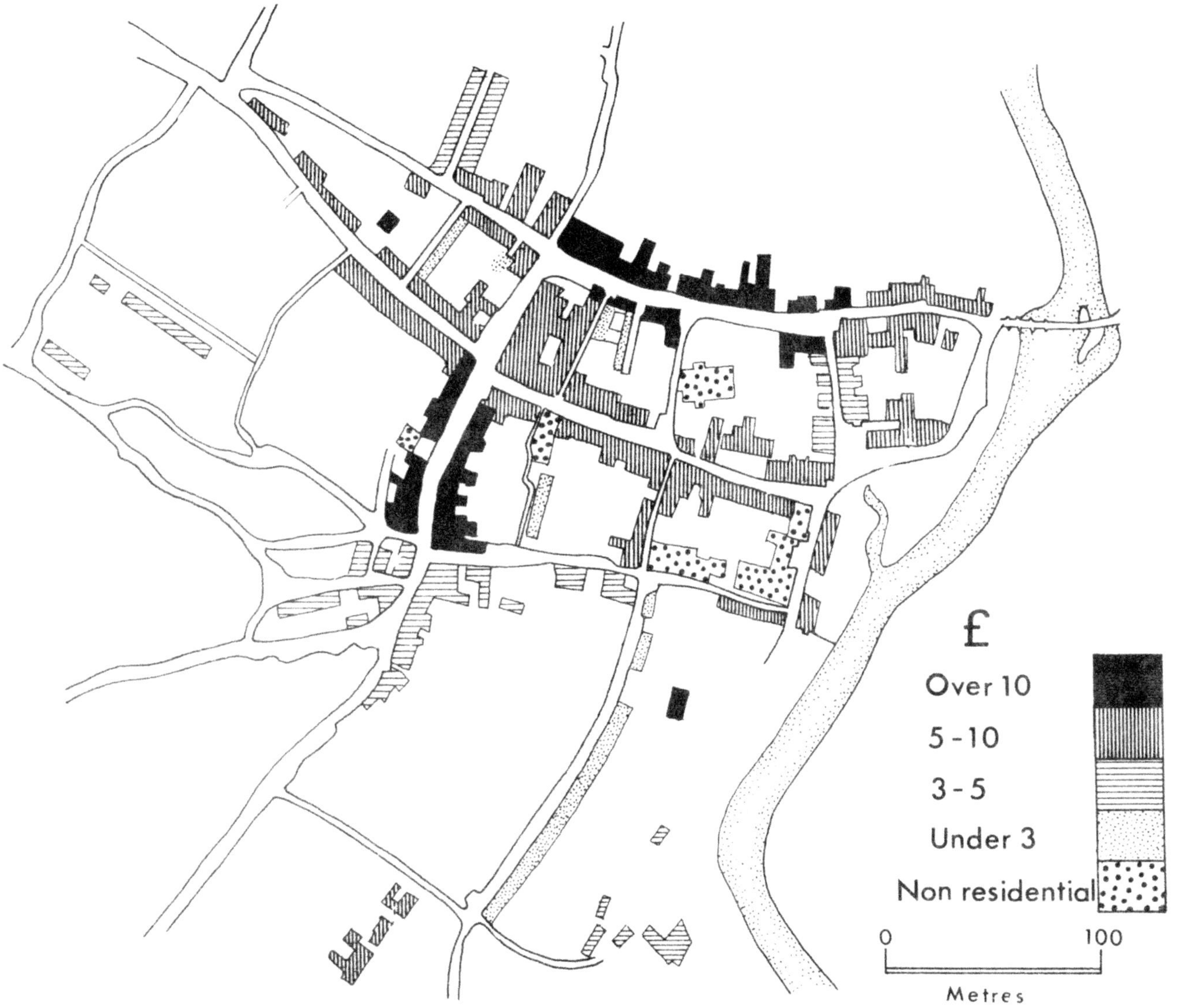

FIGURE 5

Average rateable value per house, by streets : based on the rate books for 1851

with the lists of those who held office in parish or borough, took apprentices or leased property, that the master craftsmen and prosperous shopkeepers could afford to live in houses worth £5 a year or more and that it was from this group that the churchwardens, overseers and common councillors were chosen.

Social mobility was limited. Amongst the skilled craftsmen, sons succeeded their fathers and for most of the middle class of Lostwithiel citizens, change in status or fortune was not expected and probably not wanted. It was, of course, easy enough to slide downhill, and not a few family names prominent in the borough in the eighteenth century were borne by inmates of the poor house in the early nineteenth. The Nethertons who plagued the overseers by their improvidence in the early decades of the nineteenth century, were members of a family well respected in the eighteenth.

The Fosters rose to wealth and social importance from the ranks of the skilled craftsmen. They first appeared as tanners and tanners they remained though they assumed also the mantle of merchant and banker. About 1800 they succeeded in having the poor house moved from the close proximity of their home and later in the century they moved to the rural estate of Lanwithan in St Winnow. The Norways, who had come from London in the eighteenth century, were also moving upwards socially and about 1800 built the handsome house which today looks out over the Town Quay and still bears their name.

Until well into the nineteenth century there was a limit to the pretensions of aspiring local tradesmen. Political control rested with the mayor and capital burgesses and for membership of this body the qualifications were wealth, social standing and the goodwill of the Edgcumbes. From the 1730s until 1810 its ranks were filled from the Hexts, Rashleighs, Edgcumbes and their friends. Francis Gregor, Henry Cavendish, Thomas Pitt and others who served as capital burgesses had only the most tenuous links with the borough and they valued their office only for the political power which it gave them in the election of two members of parliament. In 1810 the first breach with custom occurred; Nevil Norway was elected a capital burgess. Five years later Richard Foster was elected but it was not until 1837, when the Edgcumbes withdrew from the affairs of the borough, that the barrier between its commercial middle class and the ruling élite was broken down.

Political structure

In 1732, after many years of gross mismanagement in the affairs of the borough, a new charter was granted by George II. The old mechanism of government by mayor, capital burgesses (or aldermen) and assistants (or councillors) was perpetuated but their functions and mode of election were more clearly defined. The mayor and capital burgesses were nominated in the first instance by the charter and they were required to co-opt further members in order to fill vacancies and also each year to nominate 17 assistants or common councillors. This system survived until another - and final - charter was granted to the borough in 1886, after the parliamentary reform of municipal corporations. The system was, however, one which lent itself to grave abuse. The initial body of mayor and capital burgesses was endowed with the power to control the destinies of the borough for an indefinite period through its authority to fill its own vacancies and to nominate all members of the common council. Richard Edgcumbe, who was already Recorder of Lostwithiel, was in 1736 elected a capital burgess. Within a few years, as vacancies occurred in the ranks of the capital burgesses, friends of the Edgcumbes were elected to fill them. By the mid-century and until the Reform Bill of 1832 the Edgcumbes' control of the borough was complete. The cost to them was high but the advantages, especially to a political manipulator like the first Lord Edgcumbe, were immense.[1] The borough was represented at Westminster by two members, who were chosen by the mayor and capital burgesses. In fact they were, until the borough was disfranchised in 1832, the nominees of the Edgcumbes. The price was constant attention to the needs of the borough; the gift to it of a Guildhall, Market House and sums of money and the assumption periodically of the office of mayor. The latter was, at least for the Edgcumbes, merely honorific but it was always hoped that the incumbent mayor would underwrite any deficit in the borough's finances while in office. In this respect the Edgcumbes did not disappoint.

The political organisation of the borough underlined its social structure. The mayor and capital burgesses represented the local gentry and landowners. They were the wealthy élite and not until after the Edgcumbes had in 1837 reliquished their political interest in the borough, did they begin to co-opt the local traders and craftsmen. The minutes of the borough's Court Leet record that they registered their assent with unwavering fidelity to the acts and decisions of the capital burgesses, who were in their turn obedient to the Edgcumbes. When the latter set up their candidate for Parliament or for mayor, the seventeen went through the empty ceremony of voting unanimously for them.

The seventeen Assistants were recruited from the ranks of the more substantial traders and craftsmen. In 1841, when the council was still in large measure that which had served under the Edgcumbes, they included four drapers, three saddlers, an ironmonger, a blacksmith, a glazier and a shoemaker. These were drawn from the borough's middle class. They stood well above the poverty line and many of them were employers of labour in their shops and workplaces. Many could afford to keep a servant and they never opened their homes to lodgers. They were nominated for their office by the capital burgesses and could expect to hold it until death or old age removed them from the ranks of the assistants. Some were tenants of Edgcumbe or Hext. Many took their turn as churchwarden or overseer and in an age when most of the population was illiterate, they were as a general rule able to read and write. They were hardworking and conservative, willing to serve the political ends of their superiors, provided there were pecuniary advantages for themselves. In their quiet but persistent way they drove a hard bargain with their political masters, the Edgcumbes.

Geographical structure

Lostwithiel, it might have been supposed, was too small a town to have separate and distinct quarters in which rich and poor, traders and working-class people lived apart from one another. Far from it. The eighteenth-century borough had inherited a geographical structure in which élitist quarters stood out as clearly as those inhabited by the humblest members of Lostwithiel society. Since the middle ages

1 Lewis Namier, *The structure of politics at the accession of George III* (2nd ed. Macmillan, 1957) pp. 299-357.

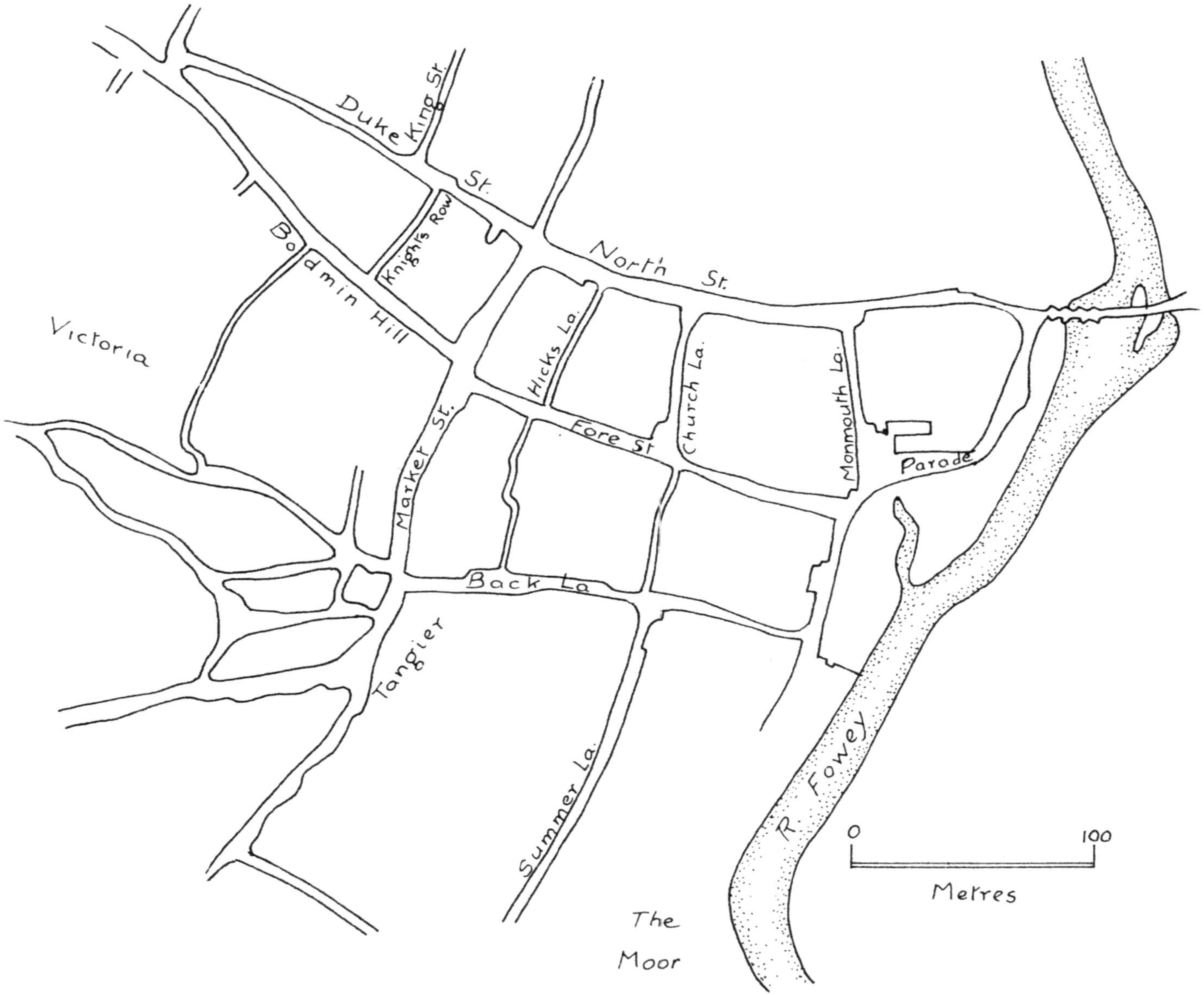

FIGURE 6

The streets of Lostwithiel, early nineteenth century

Fore Street had been the chief residential area where the leading merchants had lived. Here the Edgcumbes built their town house and opposite it the Guildhall which was their gift to the borough. Nearby were a number of large and handsome houses, most of them built by aspiring members of Lostwithiel's middle class. In the early nineteenth century, however, Fore Street appears to have been overtaken by North Street, which lay parallel to it and on the other side of the church yard. Fore Street, especially its eastern or lower end, was becoming more a street of shops and workshops than one of elegant residences. North Street, which had at one time possessed an industrial character, was rising in the social scale. Several large and elegant houses were built here and at the beginning of the nineteenth century one of them, described in Staniforth's Diary, was occupied by the Hext family.

Market Street, renamed Queen Street after the visit of Queen Victoria in 1846, was also an important commercial street and shops were also spreading up Bodmin Hill towards the large town house of the Kendalls.

The only measure of the quality of housing, apart from their physical remains, is their rateable value. The earliest surviving rate books are of 1803-5 but they list properties under the names of their occupants or owners and in most instances addresses are not given. Though many are readily identifiable, it is not practicable to locate the house of each ratepayer. Not until the mid-nineteenth century is it possible by comparing the rate books with the census books, to arrive at a picture of the quality of housing. Even so, the precision of the figures is marred by the inclusion in some of the rateable values of stables and gardens and their exclusion from others.

On this basis North Street emerges as the most highly rated street at an average of about £20 per house and is followed by Queen Street with over £15. The average rateable value of the houses in Fore Street was very little more than £8, a measure of its relative decline in social and economic significance. Nevertheless, Fore Street still contained some valuable houses, though its average value was greatly reduced by the large number of very small houses.

Fore Street and North Street are continued up the hill to the west by Bodmin Hill and Duke Street. Both contained houses with a high rateable value but were made up largely of small houses, so that their average value was respectively £5 6s and £8 2s. At the other end of the parish, close to the river, lay Quay Street, the Parade and Bridge Street. Quay Street and the Parade were a good residential area, with average values of respectively £9 15s and £7 13s 4d. The houses of Bridge Street were smaller and on average were valued at £5 6s.

Lostwithiel was in the early nineteenth century growing steadily in size, as its population figures have shown. Speculative builders erected rows of workers' cottages on what had once been burgage lots. Many of these have now disappeared; some did not outlast the nineteenth century. All were very small; most were shoddily built and some in plan and sanitary conditions cannot have been totally unlike the insanitary courts described at this time by Friedrich Engels in the northern industrial towns. Several opened off North Street: Eveleigh's Court, Teague's Court, Ward's Court, Philp's Court, each built by the entrepreneur whose name it bore. Knight's Row, demolished only in recent years, linked Duke Street with Bodmin Hill, and King Street, somewhat more solidly built, opened northwards from Duke Street. The number of houses and their average rateable value was:

Table 3

		£	s	d
King Street	21	3	4	0
Ward's Court	5	2	4	0
Eveleigh's Row	8	2	3	0
Teague's Court	5	2	15	0
Symons Court	3	2	10	0
Knight's Row	6	2	3	0

These insalubrious courts and rows were matched by the alleys which linked North Street with Fore Street. One of them, Hicks or Malthouse Lane, had the lowest average rateable value of any row in Lostwithiel parish: £2 1s. Monmouth Lane with an average of only £3, was little better.

The Lostwithiel parish rate books excluded the urban development south of the Cob brook. Few of the Lanlivery rate books have survived and the closest to that used for Lostwithiel parish is one of 1867. Most of the houses in Lanlivery Urban lay in the three clusters: Tangier, Summer Lane and Lostwithiel Moor. The 32 houses in Tangier were of very varied value, with two rated at £10 each. The average was, however, only £3 8s 3d and twenty houses were valued each at £2 10s or less. Summer Lane was even poorer. If we exclude the mansion built by Nevill Norway, which in fact stands back from the cottages of Summer Lane and was rated at £18, we have an average for 33 houses of only £2 8s 2d, as low as that of the courts and alleys off North Street. The houses on Lostwithiel Moor were more varied. They lay between Summer Lane and the river, most were mean cottages but there were amongst them some houses, perhaps with workshops attached, which were rated highly. Most however were worth less than £3. Tangier, Summer Lane and the Moor were almost exclusively working class areas. Half the heads of households in Summer Lane and the Moor were labourers or miners and most of the others - bargemen, waggoners, thatchers, lathemakers and limeburners - were at best semi-skilled.

In the early nineteenth century Lostwithiel was still in most respects a pre-industrial town. Its citizens carried on only the traditional crafts; a significant number of them practised agriculture as their chief source of livelihood and most were in some way associated with the land. The little town provided goods and services for the surrounding countryside within a radius of 5 or 6 miles, as it had done for the past five centuries. Beyond lay other small towns, with similar social structures and economic functions, protected by the short distance from the competition of Lostwithiel's market, as Lostwithiel was itself protected from them.

SECULARISATION AND THE CARE OF THE POOR IN SCOTLAND

David E Gladstone

In 1845, by the Poor Law Amendment Act, the system of poor relief in Scotland was removed from the hands of agents of the Established Church and effectively secularised. It is the contention of this paper that this occurred not so much as the result of external factors such as population growth and its regional concentration, nor of alternative theoretical analyses which assigned a less important place to religious explanations, but rather as the consequence of developing internal fragmentation within the Scottish ecclesiastical establishment itself.

I

The Scottish system for the relief of the poor, which was reformed by the Amendment Act of 1845,[1] had been in existence since an Act passed by the Scottish Parliament in 1579 'for the punishment of the strong and idle beggars and the relief of the poore and impotent'.[2] This particular piece of legislation, though described as 'the opening of a new chapter in poor law administration',[3] merely consolidated and continued a temporary Act which had been introduced five years earlier. Like the English Act of 1572, it contained elements of repression directed against those considered to be the undeserving poor. Thereafter, however, the similarities end, especially when, after less than twenty years, the agency through whom poor relief was to be administered in Scotland ceased officially to be the representatives of local government - provosts, baillies and sherrifs - and became instead the responsibility of the Established Church by whom, informally, it was already being exercised in some parishes as a Christian duty. While the English system was secular, in Scotland for two and a half centuries the administration of poor relief was inextricably bound up with the Established Church and its office-bearers. The fact that the ecclesiastical administration was already offering poor relief as 'one of the social obligations of a Christian community'[4] is, obviously, part of the explanation for the legalising of this practice in the 1590s. But it has also to be seen as part of 'the social impact of the Reformed Church'.[5] Implicit in the Book of Discipline of 1560, drawn up by John Knox and some other Calvinist reformers, were not only plans for a spiritual reformation but also a 'wider vision of a Godly Commonwealth'[6] in which the administration

1 8 and 9 Vic c LXXXIII: An act for the Amendment and Better Administration of the Laws relating to the Relief of the Poor in Scotland.

2 Acts of the Parliament of Scotland, James VI c 74 no.12, 1579.

3 Thomas Ferguson, *The dawn of Scottish social welfare: a survey from medieval times to 1863* (Nelson, 1948) p.168.

4 Rosalind Mitchison, 'The making of the old Scottish poor law', *Past and Present*, 63 (1974) 63.

5 Thomas Christopher Smout, *A history of the Scottish people 1560-1830* (Collins, 1969) p.72.

6 Smout, *Scottish people*, p.72.

of poor relief and education were to be of considerable importance in the creation of a Scottish theocracy. Though the strategy envisaged in the Book of Discipline was a national one, the policy outlined was to be primarily carried out by the parish which had been 'the Cinderella of the ecclesiastical institutions of the Middle Ages'.[1]

Parochial responsibility meant, in terms of the Presbyterian system of Church government which the Reformers had devised, that the care of the poor was entrusted to the ordained minister of the parish and an unfixed number of laymen, described in the Book of Discipline as 'men of best knowledge in God's word and cleanest life, men faithful and of the most honest conversation that can be found in the Kirk'.[2] A contributor to the *Edinburgh Review* in the mid-1830s contended that those who fulfilled these requirements came 'invariably from the most respectable classes'.[3] Quite often, if the example of Stirlingshire is typical, heritors or landowners in the district were prominent among the members, with the parochial schoolmaster, himself most usually an appointment of the Kirk Session, serving as clerk. Together the minister and such laymen comprised an executive committee of the congregation known as the Kirk Session who were responsible for the moral and spiritual well-being of the parish. In addition to their religious duties, they exercised a significant social discipline over both public and private life in the community. Bruce Lenman and Geoffrey Parker have shown the importance of the Church courts alongside the secular tribunals in the maintenance of law and order in early modern Scotland[4] while Basil Skinner and Allan MacLaren both indicate the importance of this body as an agent of significant social control in the local community which has no precise parallel in the English experience.[5]

> From 1653 to 1750 *[in the parish of St Ninians]* there were from 24 to 30 meetings of Session in the year. The ministers and elders exercised most extensive powers both in passing Acts and in punishing delinquents.
>
> Besides licentious persons, drunkards, Sabbath breakers and slanderers, they took cognisance of those guilty of theft, prevarication or perjury, of scolding and railing. Severe enactments are made against those that haunt public houses, that do not keep the Kirk and the examinations but idle persons such as vagrants and vagabonds and sturdy beggars and also those that 'resett' them, are objects of their highest displeasure.

1 John H S Burleigh, *A church history of Scotland* (Oxford University Press, 1960) p.53.

2 William Croft Dickinson, ed. *John Knox's History of the Reformation in Scotland* (2 vols. Nelson, 1949) II, Appendix VIII.

3 'Monypenny on the Scottish Poor Laws', *Edinburgh Review,* LIX (1834) 431.

4 Bruce Lenman and Geoffrey Parker, 'Law and order in early modern Scotland', *Social History Society Newsletter,* 2:1 (1977) 3.

5 Basil Skinner, 'Scottish local history: an introductory survey', *The Local Historian,* 9:7 (1971) 354; Archibald Allan MacLaren, 'Presbyterianism and the working class in a mid nineteenth century city' *[Aberdeen]*, *Scottish Historical Review,* XLVI (1967) 121.

> The elders were exhorted to see that worship was maintained in every family and great attention was paid to those who sought for baptism for their children or for admission to the Lord's Table. The education of the young was an object of peculiar care and they seem to have exercised an unlimited authority both over the teacher and his scholars. They appoint the parochial schoolmaster and allot him his salary - they instruct him what he is to teach and fix his hours of teaching, when dissatisfied call him before them, admonish, reprove or dismiss him at their pleasure.[1]

The administration of poor relief, therefore, was but one among many other social functions undertaken by the Kirk Session. The fact that it was 'a labour of love',[2] as the minister of Kilsyth described it, may have been contested by some of its administrators as well no doubt as some of its beneficiaries. But that it was 'a great labour too'[3] is shown by the following account for the parish of Balfron in the late 1830s where,

> besides exercising a minute and daily care over all the paupers on the roll, on the first Monday of every month, the minister and Kirk Session met when all the paupers who could attend were expected to make their appearance and personally to receive their monthly allowance. Those who could not appear from ill health were waited upon by some member of the Session and their condition reported. Thus was the case of every individual brought monthly under the view of the whole Session. The effects of this system of watchfulness *[continues the ministerial reporter]* were abundantly apparent. None were admitted on the roll who were not proper objects of charity. None were continued upon it who did not require relief. The poor were well attended to and contented.[4]

Not in every parish did the Kirk Session meet so frequently, make such thorough investigation of its poor nor such regular distributions of its funds. But the administrative principle was one in which over two and a half centuries local responsibility was vested in the Kirk Sessions of each of the 870 parishes in Scotland involving, at the time of the 1839 General Assembly Report, some 6000 unpaid members.[5] Even in spite of the technical constraints introduced by a judgement in the Court of Session in 1752, giving any heritor the right to call the Kirk Session

1 *The new statistical account of Scotland by the ministers of the respective parishes under the superintendence of a Committee of the Society for the Benefit of the Sons and Daughters of the Clergy* (15 vols. Edinburgh: Blackwood, 1845) VIII, 318-19.

2 Sir John Sinclair, ed. *The statistical account of Scotland drawn up from the communications of the ministers of the different parishes* (21 vols. Edinburgh, 1791-9) XVIII, 255.

3 Sinclair, *Statistical account*, XVIII, 255.

4 *New statistical account*, VIII, 300.

5 *British Parliamentary Papers (BPP)* 1839, XX: 'Report by a Committee of the General Assembly on the Management of the Poor in Scotland', p.17.

to account for their administration of the funds available for poor relief, a minister of the Church of Scotland in the early nineteenth century was still able to speak of the Kirk Sessions as being as 'equally despotic in the care of the poor as the Czar of all the Russias'.[1]

But the Scottish ecclesiastical establishment not only provided the agents by whom the system was administered: it also provided its revenue, primarily from church door collections. Together with General Sessions Funds, the amount raised for the poor in this way in the period between 1807 and 1816 was about one-third of total revenue.[2] By 1839, although the total raised by church door collections had increased by over £4000 per annum, as a proportion of total funds available it had declined to less than one quarter.[3] Other sources of specifically ecclesiastical revenue came from customary dues paid for the services of the Church at the *rites de passage* - birth, marriage and death - and by those who were brought before the Kirk Session in its role as a disciplinary body and for the more affluent of whom, in the early nineteenth century, fines came to replace the tradition of public rebuke from the pulpit. Capital sums - donations, bequests, savings and endowments - invested, on the early nineteenth-century Stirlingshire experience, in property concerns or the new road and railway developments of the period, made up the financial sources available to fund a system of relief that in much of Scotland had retained a reliance on voluntary funding. At the end of the 1830s only 236 out of the 878 Scottish parishes were rated or assessed for the relief of the poor.[4] The significance of that figure lies not so much in the small number that had introduced some regular method of providing for the poor but in the other two-thirds of the total which, in spite of industrialisation, agricultural and economic reorganisation, population migration and Irish immigration, 'places', as the 1839 General Assembly Report expressed it, 'its main reliance on the voluntary contribution of the public and never imposes a compulsory assessment so long as hopes can reasonably be entertained of procuring without it the needful assistance'.[5]

II

But what was 'needful assistance' and on what principles should it be organised? These were the issues posed at the beginning of the 1840s by the publication of a pamphlet entitled *On the management of the poor in Scotland and its effect on the health of great towns* by

1 Rev Robert Burns, cited Scottish Record Office (subsequently SRO) CH 1/2/184 General Assembly Papers, 1841. 'Second Report of the Committee of the Association for Obtaining an Official Inquiry into the Pauperism of Scotland', p.32.

2 *BPP*, 1818, V: 'Third report from the Select Committee on the Poor Laws with an Appendix containing returns from the General Assembly of the Church of Scotland', p.84.

3 *BPP*, 1839, XX, 17.

4 *BPP*, 1839, XX, 19.

5 *BPP*, 1839, XX, 4.

William Pulteney Alison. Traditionally, in the limited range of studies on the development of Scottish social welfare, Alison's role has been seen as of major significance in bringing about the Amendment Act of 1845 and the secularisation of the Scottish system of poor relief. His initial pamphlet which, in the opinion of one writer, 'opens the Poor Law Reform movement'[1] and others which he published in the early 1840s all gave voice to what has been called 'a grave indictment of the Scottish system for the care of the poor'.[2] For the previous twenty years Alison had been Professor of the Institutes of Medicine at the University of Edinburgh which, in spite of English imitations at University College, London and Manchester, was still at the beginning of the Victorian period the most important medical school in Britain and alone 'in setting medical problems in a wider social context'.[3] Though a member of the medical school, Alison had initially been trained at Edinburgh in moral philosophy under Dugald Stewart, one of the second generation of eighteenth-century literati who transmitted, especially under Whig patronage, the ideas of the social thinkers of the Scottish Enlightenment, Hume, Millar, Ferguson and Adam Smith: a short period when, in the second half of the eighteenth century, Edinburgh became known as the Athens of the North and a Mecca for budding statesmen and politicians, many of whom are known to have boarded with Stewart himself. 'A compulsive involvement in the world and a compulsive curiosity about the social sciences were perhaps', in the opinion of one recent assessment, 'in the end the best thing that the Scottish philosophers gave to the world'.[4] Each of these aspects of Scottish eighteenth-century intellectual development have implications not only for Alison's analysis of the system of poor relief but also for the secularisation of Scottish society by which 'the leaders of Scottish society became more concerned in the 18th century with economic growth, agricultural improvement and other worldly affairs than with the religious and ecclesiastical preoccupations which had dominated 17th century Scottish social history'.[5] In the universities provision for divinity students declined in relation to other disciplines. Medical education became more important than the education of ministers. And from the study of social man, that integral feature of the Scottish enlightenment, came the idea that 'the ills of the world were to be removed in life rather than compensated for in the hereafter'.[6] It is against this background that Alison's proposals for an improved system of poor relief must be set.

1 Laurence J Saunders, *Scottish democracy: the social and intellectual background 1815-1840* (Edinburgh: Oliver & Boyd, 1950) p.416.

2 Stewart Mechie, *The Church and Scottish social development 1780-1870* (Oxford University Press, 1960) p.72.

3 Michael W Flinn, ed. *Report on the sanitary condition of the labouring population of Great Britain* (Edinburgh University Press, 1965) Introduction, p.23.

4 Smout, *Scottish people*, p.482.

5 Anand Chitnis, *The Scottish enlightenment: a social history* (Croom Helm, 1976) p.155.

6 Chitnis, *Scottish enlightenment*, p.155.

His analysis began from the rising mortality of the 1830s. From a death rate of 25 per thousand in Edinburgh in the decade between 1810 and 1819, the figure had increased to 29 per thousand in the 1830s.[1] Part of this was explained by the recurrence of fever but the significance of Alison's work, based on his position as Physician to the New Town Dispensary in Edinburgh from its foundation in 1815 to give relief to the sick and diseased poor, was that:

> for the extension of epidemic disease the most influential of all causes is Poverty and Destitution . . . it is among those of the poor who suffer the greatest deprivations - whose employment is precarious, often suspended or little profitable, and among disabled men, 'lone' women, widows and orphans and especially among the poor Irish that fever most frequently appears and always spreads itself most rapidly and extensively.[2]

Identifying the problem in terms of need unrelieved, the uncertainty, inadequacy and irregularity of the relief that was given, Alison was severely critical of the existing system of parish management.

> Our concern [he wrote] is with a country in which the parochial management in most districts is such that the great body are in a miserable state of destitution and are left dependent for their subsistence either on certain voluntary charitable institutions, or more frequently on the charity of their neighbours nearly as poor as themselves, or on common begging.[3]

He produced figures which showed the small allowance given by each Kirk Session to the poor in Scotland compared with that given in England. In this he had the support of many medical practitioners who gave evidence to the Royal Commission on the Scottish Poor Laws which reported in 1844.[4] To deny relief or to give inadequate relief on the assumption that the aim of the system, as contended by many of its defenders, was support and not maintenance, Alison argued, was merely to encourage the destitution which in many cases engendered disease.

His criticism sprang not only from his interest as a student of medicine in a quest for the origin of disease. He was also a product of the Enlightenment and as such central to his criticism was the fact that the changed conditions of Scottish society required a revised system to provide an adequate assistance to the poor.

1 John H P Brotherton, *Observations on the early public health movement in Scotland* (H K Lewis & Co, 1952) p.47.

2 William P Alison, *Observations on the management of the poor in Scotland and its effect on the health of great towns* (Edinburgh, 1840) p.15.

3 William P Alison, *Remarks on the Report of Her Majesty's Commissioners on the Poor Laws of Scotland* (Edinburgh, 1844) p.49.

4 *BPP*, 1844, XX: 'Report from Her Majesty's Commissioners for inquiring into the administration and practical operation of the Poor Laws in Scotland'.

> In a perfectly simple and at the same time educated and civilised state of society [Alison pointed out in phrases redolent of some of his Enlightenment mentors] where all the higher orders who are to give and all the lower orders who are to receive are aware of their duties and are known to one another, and as long as the proprietors are resident, of charitable disposition and attentive to their duties, the burdens may be sufficiently equalised among the former and the benefits sufficiently secured to the latter without the intervention of the law.[1]

But Scottish society, he contended, was no longer like that. With better transport, agricultural improvement and greater wealth, the practice had developed towards the end of the eighteenth century of landowners spending increasing periods away from their estates in either Edinburgh or London. Such a practice had obvious implications for a system of poor relief heavily dependent on voluntary contributions. 'Your want of funds', the Kirk Session of Campsie was informed in 1823, 'is entirely owing to the non resident heritors not making payment of their subscriptions'.[2] In the neighbouring parish of Kilsyth 'where most of the heritors do not reside' the minister stated in his contribution to Sinclair's *Statistical account* that 'the sums collected for the poor have been collected literally from the poor, or from the lower orders of the people, that is from farmers, tradesmen and the few residing heritors who attend the Established church'.[3]

The finance available for poor relief was conditioned not only by the practice of heritors spending periods away from their estates. It was also affected by the extent to which the landowner came to espouse the principles of Scottish Episcopalianism. The repeal of the penal laws in 1792,[4] the progressive Anglicisation of the upper classes and the habit of sending their sons to English public schools, together with the Romantic movement epitomised by Sir Walter Scott and the dissension within the Church of Scotland itself, all contributed to a situation which favoured membership of the Episcopal Church. Between 1838 and 1858 its congregations increased from 75 to 150 and its clergy from 78 to 163.[5] Possessing only six or seven congregations in Glasgow and the west of Scotland at the beginning of the 1830s, by 1843 a further seven had been established. While its membership was drawn from all social classes,[6] it was its attraction for the heritors that most disconcerted the clergy of the

1 Alison, *Observations on the management of the poor*, p.58.

2 SRO, CH 2/51/3 Kirk Session Records, Campsie, 1823.

3 Sinclair, *Statistical account*, XVIII, 257.

4 For a recent discussion, see Frederick C Mather, 'Church, Parliament and penal laws: some Anglo-Scottish interactions in the eighteenth century', *English Historical Review*, XCII (1977) 540-72.

5 Frederick Goldie, *A short history of the Episcopal Church in Scotland* (SPCK, 1951) p.88.

6 See Barbara M Thatcher, 'The Episcopal Church in Helensburgh in the mid-nineteenth century' in John Butt and John T Ward, ed. *Scottish themes: essays in honour of Professor S G E Lythe* (Edinburgh: Scottish Academic Press, 1976) p.110.

Established Church. Several of them commented on its adverse effect on funds available for the poor and one clergyman in Stirlingshire saw it as worthy of comment that one heritor of the Scottish Episcopal Church had given a donation of one hundred guineas to the parish poor fund.

> 'He saw and had the humanity to acknowledge [the minister continued] that the poor of the parish suffered a loss by his absence and when he gave the sum he said 'he was only paying what he owed them'.[1]

Important as these factors are, reflecting as they do considerable socio-economic changes in Scottish society, the secularisation of the care of the poor was due, in addition, to other aspects of the developing plurality of religious experience in nineteenth-century Scotland.

III

The clergy of the Established Church were against the extension of legal provision for the poor through the introduction of assessment or rating which was at the base of Alison's proposals for reform in order to combat 'the misery, degradation and mendicity which are now so prevalent'[2] and to provide an adequate assistance to those in need. A firmer financial foundation for relief, they argued, would merely create a condition of increased dependency. This is a sense in which it seemed that the early nineteenth-century Scottish Church 'had swallowed whole the concepts of a laissez-faire economy and Malthusian dogma'[3] but it may have been also a reflection of Evangelical ascendancy with its emphasis on individual - not social - salvation.

It is not surprising, therefore, that many of the clergy writing the reports on their parishes for the *New statistical account* published in the mid-1840s - the time when the debate about reform was gathering momentum - were concerned to emphasise the success of the traditional system and to criticise nothing except the idea of assessment.

> Of all the public funds in Europe [the minister of one Stirlingshire parish pointed out] none is managed with so little expense to the fund itself, none so frugally, none so impartially and none is laid out more to the purpose for which they were raised than the poor's fund under the care of the Kirk Sessions of Scotland.[4]

Another local minister described the Scottish system as 'the cheapest, best managed, public fund in Great Britain'.[5] Nationally, Sir John Sinclair, analysing clerical returns, concluded that the opinion of the clergy was 'greatly in favour of the primitive mode of relieving the poor'.[6] And the

1 Sinclair, *Statistical account*, XVIII, 113.

2 'Second Report of the Committee of the Association for Obtaining an Official Inquiry into the Pauperism of Scotland', p. 51.

3 Mitchison, 'The making of the old Scottish poor law', p.92.

4 *New statistical account*, VIII, 301.

5 *New statistical account*, VIII, 363.

6 Sir John Sinclair, *Analysis of the statistical account of Scotland* (2 vols. John Murray, 1826) II, 165.

two *Reports of the General Assembly of the Church of Scotland* published in 1818 and 1839 similarly reasserted the validity of the traditional method.

If Alison's analysis and recommendations for reform were based on the idea of a changing socio-economic structure, the clergy's attempt was more than an unconscious philosophy of reaction - though clerical opinion on other issues at this time did tend also to be conservative. It was also an attempt to prevent the secularisation of the care of the poor and an attempt to preserve the pattern of traditional Scotland in the changed conditions of an increasingly industrialised society. And, some would argue, that since the Church was an element of continuing cultural identity guaranteed, like the legal system and education, by the Act of Union of 1707 so there was, in the clerical defence of the traditional system of poor relief, which it had operated, what can be regarded as elements of nationalism and Anglophobia. These elements of clerical defence were expressed most forcefully by the Rev Dr Thomas Chalmers, an influential figure in the Evangelical Party of the Church of Scotland which, in the 1830s, gained the ascendancy over the Moderates who had dominated ecclesiastical thought and policy in Scotland through most of the eighteenth century. For Chalmers and many of his clerical contemporaries, the changed conditions of Scottish society, which had occurred especially in the western Lowlands and the central belt, had not so much created the conditions for a re-assessment of the administrative structure of poor relief but rather produced a challenge to the Church to recreate in the urban centres of population concentration the ethos of community or, as Perkin has termed it, 'the paternalism of the country village'.[1] Not uninfluenced by his first ministerial charge at Kilmany, a rural parish in Fife, Chalmers believed that even in the vastly different conditions of the Tron parish in Glasgow, to which he was inducted in 1815, the 'principle of locality' could become operational and that:

> the old paternal order could be restored and maintained . . . if only the Church could divide its old parishes into smaller more manageable units, take the central place in every parish in the land, and by its ministers, teachers, elders, deacons and other workers bring personal contact, spiritual and moral teaching, and, in the case of need, financial help to the whole population.[2]

For Chalmers the aim was to re-awaken in the industrial areas the spirit of local kindness and voluntary assistance - in essence the traditional method of relief - which, by this time, was almost exclusively limited to parishes outside the urban centres. Against the legal system where it existed for the dependent pauperism which it created, Chalmers believed that the Church could play, through a programme of new building, a more adequate pastoral superintendence and a reform of parochial units as envisaged in his 'principle of locality', an important role in creating the conditions favourable to the transition from what he termed 'the charity of human laws to the charity of human kindness'.[3]

1 Harold Perkin, *The origins of modern English society 1780-1880* (Routledge & Kegan Paul, 1969) p.445.

2 Mechie, *Church and Scottish social development,* p. 55.

3 Thomas Chalmers, *The Christian and civic economy of large towns* (3 vols. Glasgow, 1821-6) II, 55.

The idea of the Church in the centre of the community, and operating in the way in which Chalmers envisaged, was one that had suffered consequent on the changes in Scottish society created by the process of industrialisation and population mobility and immigration. The religious consequences of this process were repeatedly referred to but a Pastoral Letter to the General Assembly in 1835 summed up the situation:

> The result of all our inquiries impresses upon us more and more the appalling consideration that in all the most populous districts of the kingdom, multitudes are pressing on towards eternity in utter ignorance of the way of salvation and many thousands of children are growing up to manhood without being brought up in the nurture and admonition of the Lord and we dare not acquit ourselves of the guilt of having failed to provide the means which it might have been in the power of our hand to employ, for averting or removing these growing evils.[1]

The main method of averting or removing these growing evils, to which the Pastoral Letter referred, was the policy of Church extension. A Committee for this purpose had been established by the General Assembly in 1828 but it was not until 1834, when Chalmers was appointed its Convenor, that it began to show significant results. At the close of his first year as Convenor he was able to report to the Assembly that over £66,000 had been raised and that 64 churches were in the process of being built. By 1840 this number had increased to 216.[2]

For Chalmers himself, the purpose behind all the activity was clear. It was that:

> through the multiplication of endowed Churches and schools the common people of Scotland may again become what they were in other days, the best taught, the most religious and, as an unfailing consequence of this, the freest from all the vices of pauperism and the most independent peasantry in Europe.
>
> In the practical wisdom of our Scottish Church there lies a secret which has baffled the whole practical economy of the English Parliament, the elevation of character by spiritual forces as opposed to the materialism of benevolence.[3]

Not only is it possible to criticise Chalmers' position as one concerned more with pauperism than with poverty. His aspirations for re-Christianising industrial Scotland also failed to take into account two other important factors. Of these the first was the number of the non-Church-going. By the 1830s, according to evidence presented to the

1 SRO, Acts of the General Assembly 1835, p.45, cited Andrew L Drummond and James Bulloch, *The Scottish Church, 1688-1843: the age of the moderates* (Edinburgh: Saint Andrew Press, 1973) p. 230.

2 SRO, CH 1/2/184: Seventh Report of the Committee of the General Assembly of the Church of Scotland on church extension, p.17.

3 SRO, CH 1/2/184, p.21.

General Assembly, the number of the non-church-going in Edinburgh and Glasgow had reached approximately 100,000.[1] For them the problem was not only that of inadequate church accommodation, as several clerical commentators interpreted it at that time.[2] But Chalmers also failed fully to appreciate the implications of the increase of dissent in Scotland.

The extent of dissent from the established Presbyterian fabric was obviously an important factor in a system of poor relief that relied for its administration on an agency of the Established Church and for its funds on church door collections and other voluntary sources in the considerable number of parishes where no assessment was levied. While practice seems to have varied both as to whether the poor of dissenting congregations were relieved by parish funds and whether such congregations made any contribution to monies available for relief, the spread of dissent within the Presbyterian fabric by the early part of the nineteenth century posed considerable strains to the administrative principles on which the scheme was organised. Setting aside the question of the Irish immigrant poor which was itself quite significant,[3] the Royal Commission on Religious Instruction in Scotland appointed in 1835 to 'inquire into the opportunities for public religious worship and means of religious instruction and pastoral superintendence afforded to the people of Scotland' showed that in some parishes the proportion of those belonging to denominations other than the Established Church was as high as 40 per cent.[4]

The internal splintering of the Presbyterian fabric had been intermittently in progress since the Secession led by Ebenezer Erskine in 1733 created the First or Original Secession Church but disputes over patronage, especially in the presentation of ministers to parishes by heritors or landowners, led to the increasing challenge of statute law as the Evangelical Party gained ascendancy in the General Assembly. Decisions of the General Assembly were pronounced *ultra vires* by the civil courts which finally led, in 1843, to the decision by a considerable minority, who rejected lay interference in what they regarded as spiritual concerns, to renounce the State connection and form the Free Church of Scotland. 451 ministers, over one-third of the clerical strength of the Church, signed the deed of demission and within eight years, at the Religious Census of 1851, the Church of Scotland nationally only narrowly beat the Free Church on attendance figures. By the same date, in at least one city, Aberdeen, 'the Free Church . . . had clearly established itself . . . as the largest single denomination'.[5] With wealthy and influential support

1 SRO, Acts of the General Assembly, 1838, p.43.

2 See, for example, Sinclair, *Statistical account*, VIII, 292-3; *New statistical account*, VIII, 200; SRO CH 1/2/184: Report on the proposed inquiry into the state of the poor in Scotland presented to the General Assembly in 1841, pp.8-9.

3 James E Handley, *The Irish in Scotland 1798-1845* (Cork University Press, 1943).

4 SRO HH 37: Royal Commission on religious instruction in Scotland, 1835. See, eg, HH 37/60: Returns from parishes of St Ninians and Stirling.

5 Archibald Allan MacLaren, *Religion and social class: the Disruption years in Aberdeen* (Routledge & Kegan Paul, 1974) p.100.

it was able to erect churches and schools throughout Scotland in something like a duplication of the entire ecclesiastical and educational structure. It is curiously ironic that it was Chalmers, by now playing the role of the ecclesiastical politician, who led that movement out from the Church of Scotland, which was to prove the most numerically and socially significant of all such attempts over the previous century.

By the Disruption of 1843, as the recent historians of the Church in Victorian Scotland have pointed out,

> the Church, which once had represented the whole nation had sunk to a position not so very different from that of a private religious society. [1]

While it may not conform in every terminological detail used by sociologists of religion, it is possible to see in the Disruption something of the process of the denominationalisation of the Scottish ecclesiastical establishment in which, while the Church of Scotland retained the particular privileges of establishment, its role, more so than hitherto, especially in numerical terms, was cast in a situation of Presbyterian plurality. In that kind of situation it had lost a base of credibility from which to continue to act as an effective agent of social welfare. The effect of the Disruption was that it 'virtually sealed the fate of the old poor law . . . and made it unworkable'.[2]

IV

The Scottish Poor Law Amendment Act reached the Statute Book in 1845. Like the *Report of the Royal Commission* which had preceded it, it was in its proposals for administrative reorganisation that the Act was most innovatory.[3] It introduced in Edinburgh a central Board of Supervision, without an ecclesiastical representative, to which was assigned the duty of general oversight of the operation of the Poor Law and over the Parochial Boards upon whom rested the responsibility for its local administration. Although there were some technical constraints on its functions, by directive, report, review of inadequate relief and personal inspection, the conditions had been created for the development of a strong centralised agency where none had hitherto existed.

But perhaps the greatest administrative change occurred at the parish level, especially in membership of Parochial Boards. In parishes

1 Drummond and Bulloch, *The Scottish Church*, p. 177.

2 William Ferguson, *Scotland 1689 to the present* (Edinburgh: Oliver & Boyd, 1968) p.313.

3 For a discussion of the poor law in Scotland after 1845 see Audrey Paterson, 'The poor law in nineteenth century Scotland' in Derek Fraser, ed. *The new poor law in the nineteenth century* (Macmillan, 1976) pp.171-93. Also David E Gladstone, 'The new poor law in Scotland: the administrative reorganisation of the first quinquennium', *Social and Economic Administration*, 9 (1975) 115-27.

which continued to rely on voluntary funds for the relief of the poor, the administration remained in the hands of members of Kirk Sessions, heritors and magistrates although the number of eligible heritors increased after the legislation of 1845 under the new property qualifications. But given that in the revised system the facility existed for a pauper formally to complain to the Board of Supervision about inadequate relief - a facility which over 3000 had used by 1850 - the number of parishes which relied exclusively on voluntary funds considerably declined. At the beginning of the 1840s the number of assessed parishes in Scotland was 236 out of a total of 878 parishes. By 1850 there were only 230 parishes remaining unassessed, a figure which had declined to 46 by the next reform of the system of poor relief by the Local Government Act of 1894. Where an assessment was introduced, elected representatives of the ratepayers - usually the largest group - formed part of the membership of Parochial Boards along with representatives of the Kirk Sessions and either magistrates in burghs or heritors in rural areas. In these ways, therefore, largely in consequence of a changed interpretation of the nature of relief - seen after 1845 as maintenance rather than as a support to be combined with other voluntary forms of family and community assistance - the administrative structure relating to poor relief significantly altered.

V

In looking at the legislation of 1845 historians of Scottish social policy have tended to see in it simply a victory for Alison and the medical interest over an unsuccessful rearguard action fought by the clergy of the Established Church as part of its attempt to retain the distinctiveness of a national institution in the vastly changed conditions of an industrial society. In part this analysis is in agreement with that traditional interpretation. But that view has not hitherto explained how it was that Alison's critique and proposals became the basis of the legislation passed in 1845. This is not only intelligible in terms of the changing intellectual climate within Scotland in the second half of the eighteenth century and the early nineteenth century in which a plurality of views competed more or less on equal terms. It has to be seen also by reference to an examination of the internal structure of the religious establishment itself. Not only did it find itself functioning in a different social, economic and political milieu - each of them important factors in our analysis: it also suffered in this period significant internal fragmentation.

To the changed society the moderate domination of the Church of Scotland had shown itself, in the second half of the eighteenth century, more capable of adaptation and possibly, therefore, somewhat incongruously of continuing as a national establishment in matters of poor relief and education. It was the Evangelicals, even more incongruously, standing for conservative presbyterian and puritan values and seeking to retain the traditional forms of Scottish society who, as they gained ascendancy in the General Assembly in the 1830s, created the conditions of theological principle which made their plans for the maintenance of the traditional system of poor relief an impossibility. Marwick argued that 'the secularisation of the care of the poor deprived the Church of much of its direct influence on social life'.[1] But the Church not only experienced the effect of that process: it was itself a significant cause of the secularisation of social welfare in nineteenth-century Scotland.

1 William H Marwick, *Economic developments in Victorian Scotland* (Allen & Unwin, 1936) p. 231.

UNEMPLOYMENT RELIEF WORKS IN SOUTHAMPTON BETWEEN THE WARS: A CASE STUDY

Adrian J Vinson

The 'Chamberlain circular' of 1886 and the Unemployed Workmen's Act of 1905 gave new impetus to the case for publicly-funded relief works, as opposed to maintenance allowances, for the unemployed. Though marking a significant stage in the acceptance of national responsibilities, these measures relied, as had earlier initiatives, on the administrative machinery and largely the financial resources of local authorities. By contrast, the commitment in the Development Act of 1909 to the promotion of counter-depression works was to be nationally administered and funded. So too were the Liberal experiments in the provision of maintenance outside the moral taint of the Poor Law under Part II of the 1911 National Insurance Act, operating within the framework of an attempt to equate the supply of and demand for labour under the Labour Exchanges Act of 1909.

Before the first world war, the merits of rationalisation of the labour market combined with maintenance through insurance had apparently supplanted faith in relief works as the principal remedies for unemployment. José Harris states furthermore that, 'by 1908-9 it was therefore widely accepted by politicians and administrators that, whatever kind of remedial policy was adopted, it should be national rather than local in its organisation and aims'.[1] This paper examines, through the focus of one locality,[2] the impact of post-war unemployment of unprecedented severity on the case for publicly-funded works and on the relationship between national and local agencies with regard to their implementation.

1 José F Harris, *Unemployment and politics* (Oxford University Press, 1972) p. 348.

2 While the boundaries of a county borough, especially of a port, cannot define the economic, social, political or even administrative horizons of its citizens, they nonetheless provide the most relevant unit for the purposes of this paper. The boundaries of the County Borough of Southampton were extended in November 1920 by the annexation of the parishes of St Nicholas, Bitterne and Itchen, doubling the area of the borough to make it co-terminous with the two-member Parliamentary constituency. (For population statistics, see Appendix 2, Table A.) Poor Law responsibility for these parishes was transferred from the South Stoneham Union to the Southampton Union in April 1924. The concentration of the shipbuilding and ship-repairing industries, with their high levels of unemployment, in the Woolston district east of the river Itchen, gave special significance to the boundary extension in the 1920s and 1930s.

I

Unemployment in Southampton between the wars corresponded fairly closely to the national average,[1] with the one qualification that the full impact of the trade cycle lagged by about a year behind its national incidence. Southampton's economic structure,[2] and consequently her pattern of employment and unemployment, were in a number of respects a microcosm of the national economy. As Britain's 'Premier Passenger Port' Southampton was dominated by a group of staple industries. Even in 1937 the docks, shipping, shipbuilding and ship-repairing employed 35 per cent of the insured population.[3] Although the expansion of the port in the 1920s was more pronounced and its contraction in the early 1930s less severe than that of its northern counterparts, these industries which were nationally amongst the most depressed were locally responsible for over 50 per cent of unemployment during the Slump. In addition to a high level of structural unemployment and a marked responsiveness to cyclical factors, the port industries' traditional pattern of seasonal and casual employment persisted throughout the inter-war period in spite of periodic decasualisation schemes. In the late 1920s casuals formed 39-68 per cent of the live register of unemployed, according to season.[4] Inevitably the special problems of the port industries were a major factor in local attitudes to unemployment policy.

If the staple port industries were an unstable source of employment in Southampton, other activities, locally as nationally, experienced growth during the period as a whole. Service industries benefitted from the passenger trade and the requirements of a hinterland

1 For national and local unemployment statistics, see Appendix 2, Tables B - E. Differences in the official bases of compilation tend to exaggerate the percentage of local unemployment by comparison to the national figures. Thus these statistics, though comparable for trend, cannot provide a precise comparison of absolute levels of local and national unemployment at particular points in time.

2 For Southampton's occupational structure, see Appendix 1. This section is substantially based on information derived from Percy Ford, *Work and wealth in a modern port* (Allen & Unwin, 1934) especially chapters III and IV; Michael P Fogarty, *Prospects of the industrial areas of Great Britain* (Methuen, 1945) pp. 410-16; and papers deposited in the Southampton Record Office by Sir James Matthews, CBE (DZ 72).

3 Calculated from the Minutes of Evidence of the Ministry of Labour to *The Royal Commission on the Geographical Distribution of the Industrial Population*, Non-Parliamentary papers 1938, Appendix I, Table xxxii, p. 314.

6 Calculated from the weekly statistics of the Local Employment Exchange published in the *Southern Daily Echo*, 1926-8. Despite a decasualisation scheme formulated in 1916 and revised in 1925, the growth of trade in the 1920s and the tendency of surplus labour to gravitate towards the docks, enhanced in the mid-1920s by the relaxation of Unemployment Insurance regulations relating to casual employment, led to an expansion of the number of tallies issued from 2500 in 1919 to 3000 in 1927.

covering much of Hampshire. Construction and utility industries participated in the housing boom in the late 1920s and a series of prestige projects in the 1930s. The construction industries, however, shared with the port industries a degree of labour intensiveness, a seasonal pattern of demand and a casual mode of employment which rendered building workers second only to ship-repairers as the subject of specific concern.

Like the national economy, Southampton also had its 'new' manufacturing industries. A nucleus of marine engineering was extended shortly before the war by the advent of Pirelli's cable works and supplemented in the 1920s by the production of motor vehicles and aircraft and by oil refining and in the 1930s by a range of light consumer industries attracted by Southampton's transport facilities and proximity to the markets of London and the south-east. Though the southward drift of industry and the growth of the passenger trade were the cause of much optimism for Southampton's economic prospects between the wars,[1] it is evident from the unemployment statistics that these developments were insufficient to eliminate the incidence of structural, let alone seasonal, casual and cyclical unemployment.

II

If Southampton's economic structure larely determined the nature of her unemployment problems, the structure of municipal politics underwent a change in 1920 which was to influence local attitudes towards the mitigation of unemployment throughout the period. In that year a group of councillors, reacting against the autocratic domination of civic affairs by a Conservative caucus yet opposed to Labour 'extremism', launched in consultation with the Southampton Ratepayers' Association, a 'non-party platform' of which economical administration and rate reduction were the central planks.[2] A year later the Independents, now comprising all members of Council outside the Labour Group, claimed to have achieved 'more united and earnest work in the interests of the ratepayers'.[3] Though Labour formed the dominant element on the Southampton Board of Guardians from 1919 to 1922 and held the two-member Parliamentary constituency from 1929 to 1931, the Independents achieved a substantial success in preventing Labour control of the Council between the wars.[4] Labour's minority status was reinforced by tight Independent control over aldermanic seats, committee chairmanships and the influential General Purposes Committee - precisely the tactics condemned in their Conservative predecessors. While there was some truth in Independent allegations of the monolithic nature of the Labour vote on most issues, there was also validity in Labour's claim that the Independents, amongst whom Liberals were in any case a small and diminishing presence, had inherited the Conservative caucus system.

1 *The Hampshire Advertiser*, for instance, commented on 28 December 1929, 'Southampton has reason to look ahead with some complacency'.

2 *Hampshire Independent*, 6 March, 3 April, 11 September 1920.

3 *Hampshire Advertiser*, 24 September 1921.

4 See Appendix 3.

The resulting polarisation of political attitudes was enhanced by a conflict of personalities between the Labour leader throughout the inter-war years, Tommy Lewis,[1] and the 'dominant personality' of Alderman Sidney Kimber, leader of the Independents from their formation to 1934.[2] In the absence of a dominant Town Clerk, local politics had a somewhat negative stamp, continuity being derived largely from the determination of the Independent majority, unified primarily in their concern for the rates, to keep Labour from office. In the 1930s Southampton's local government came in for severe criticism both in the national press[3] and from the borough's Conservative MP, William Craven-Ellis, who commented that 'the Corporation are very enterprising when they are not quarrelling, but they are always quarrelling so there is no enterprise'.[4]

III

At the Armistice, locally as nationally, post-war unemployment was anticipated as a largely transitional phenomenon. The appropriate remedies were therefore seen as temporary measures, concentrating not on the need for any net addition to the demand for labour but rather on the one hand on ensuring a relatively liberal entitlement to maintenance for the transitional period through the introduction of Out-of-Work Donations and on the other hand on maximising the efficiency of the labour market for the absorption of demobilised or displaced labour. In Southampton this task was complicated by the town's status as a disembarkation point and by 'deplorable congestion' in the docks prior to the completion of demilitarisation of the port in November 1920.

In both functions the principal agency was the Local Employment Exchange, with its advisory bodies, the Local Employment Committee formed by the Ministry of Labour in 1917 from representatives of employers and workpeople under an independent chairman and the Advisory Committee on Juvenile Employment established by the Borough Council's Education Committee under the Choice of Employment Act, 1910.

1 Thomas Lewis, CBE (1873-1962): Labour member of Southampton Borough Council 1901-61, during most of which period he was Leader of the Labour Group and a prominent member of Southampton Trades Council. MP for Southampton 1929-31 and 1945-50. An active member of the Friendly Society movement and an honorary officer of the British Seafarers' Union 1911-28. For further biographical details see Joyce M Bellamy and John Saville, *Dictionary of Labour Biography, Volume I* (Macmillan, 1972) pp. 215-16.

2 Sir Sidney Guy Kimber (1873-1949): a member of Southampton Borough Council from 1910-48, first as a Conservative and subsequently as an Independent. Mayor 1918-20. Brickmaker. See Sir Sidney G Kimber, *Thirty-eight years in public life in Southampton* (Southampton: the author, 1949). Kimber's somewhat abrasive personality was the cause not only of antipathetic relations between the party leaders but of periodic friction within the Independent party, culminating in Kimber's displacement as party leader in 1934.

3 Clough Williams-Ellis, writing in the *Saturday Review* on 7 February 1931, accused Southampton's local government of: 'muddle and make-believe, incompetence and eyewash, or Bumbledown and Bombast' (quoted in the *Hampshire Advertiser*, 14 March 1931).

4 *Southern Daily Echo*, 22 December 1937.

From the outset the effectiveness of the Local Employment Committee was subject to both internal and external constraints. Poor attendance, arbitrary co-options and rivalry between unions and districts soon convinced the Ministry of Labour that Southampton's was 'a somewhat weak Committee'.[1] Despite its concern for the employment of ex-servicemen, the Committee, no doubt reflecting the fears of both employers and unions for the threat to the status quo represented by demobilised men, strenuously resisted the Ministry's efforts to appoint military representatives to the Committee and requests for the direct representation of discharged soldiers and sailors. The increasing organisation and militancy of the latter, however, led the Committee to reconsider its position in October 1919. The number of ex-servicemen on the live register of the unemployed rose to 1100 by Christmas 1920 and 2400 in 1922. The Committee's attempts to embrace civilian casualties of demobilisation, and in particular to expand the range of employment opportunities for women, brought further conflict with the Discharged Soldiers and Sailors Association, protesting at the employment of 400 women scraping ships' bottoms while men were idle.[2] Throughout 1920 and 1921 there were some 500 women on Southampton's live register.

Employment opportunities for those under the age of 18, liable to bear much of the brunt of the disruptive effects of demobilisation, were the principal concern of the Juvenile Advisory Committee. By late 1920, 248 boys were taking advantage of the government's Interrupted Apprenticeship Training Scheme.[3] Efforts to develop private apprenticeship schemes to discourage boys from seeking dead-end or casual jobs were constrained by trade union reservations accentuated by rising unemployment. During a boilermakers' strike in 1923 the local Shipbuilding and Engineering Federation accused the Advisory Committee of creating unemployment amongst journeymen by stocking firms with apprentices.[4] A sample survey in 1923 indicated that 17 per cent of boys and 24 per cent of girls had waited over 12 months for work.[5] Though the Borough Council agreed early in 1923 to establish a Juvenile Unemployment Centre for 600 juveniles on the live register, one councillor objected that 'it was educating boys to be gentlemen while there was no room for any more gentlemen in the country' and an alderman enquired rhetorically as to whether it was suggested that the town should give money to keep boys off the streets. A centre for girls was rejected as there was plenty to occupy them at home.[6]

1 PRO LAB 2/375. Of the Woolston Sub-Committee, the Employment Exchange Manager reported in October 1920 that 'consequent upon the non-attendance and lack of interest of the majority of members, no action has been possible to stimulate local authorities and employers in the development of industry'.

2 *Hampshire Independent*, 28 June 1919. The National Association of Discharged Soldiers and Sailors claimed 1500 local members and the Comrades of the Great War 1350.

3 *Hampshire Independent*, 23 October 1920.

4 *Hampshire Advertiser*, 29 September 1923.

5 *Hampshire Advertiser*, 19 January 1924.

6 *Hampshire Independent*, 20 April 1923. The Education Committee had opposed the proposal on the grounds of cost, despite the availability of a 75 per cent grant from the Ministry of Labour.

It was evident by the early 1920s that efforts to facilitate reconstruction through the existing mechanisms of the labour market had met with only very limited success, in part reflecting institutional inadequacies in circumstances beyond the envisaged scope of the Employment Exchange system and in part a variety of vested interests. The emergence of mass unemployment in 1920, by casting grave doubts on the efficacy of rationalisation as a cure, placed renewed emphasis on alternative policies including the advocacy of publicly-funded relief works.

IV

Demobilisation again supplied the stimulus, prompting from February 1919 requests for the promotion of relief works by Borough Council and Boards of Guardians from the Local Employment Committee, the Local Government Board and its successor the Ministry of Health, the Ministry of Transport and in January 1921 the newly-appointed Unemployment Grants Committee, the latter two offering the carrot of grant aid for local authority work advanced on account of unemployment. The stick was wielded by local bodies, beginning in June 1919 with a demand from the Discharged Soldiers and Sailors Association for work in place of Out-of-Work Donations condemned as charity no better than the workhouse.[1] Demands for work were accentuated by the cessation of Donations for civilians in November 1919 and for ex-servicemen in April 1921. As unemployment escalated, ex-service organisations claiming by February 1921 to represent 4000 demobilised unemployed sent deputations to Council and Guardians. The rejection of their request for direct representation on the Council led to the nomination of ex-service candidates in municipal elections, the British Legion winning a by-election in 1923.

The Local Employment Committee's growing recognition that rising unemployment was unamenable to their own unaided efforts resulted in December 1920 in a deputation to submit a list of relief schemes for expedition by Council, together with appeals to private property owners and the Railway Company. In addition to the traditional preference of its trade union members for work before maintenance, the Employment Committee as an agency of the Ministry of Labour was no doubt anxious to minimise the tax burden arising from Donations and Unemployment Insurance. For the Boards of Guardians, alarmed at rising out-relief expenditure, the attractions of relief work financed jointly by government grants and the borough (rather than the poor) rate, were more direct. Though the Southampton Guardians, influenced by Labour as the largest united group on the Board between 1919 and 1922, attempted to give substance to their preference for work over out-relief through employment on Poor Law properties,[2] their own capacity to generate work was very limited. The Board periodically asserted national responsibility for the financial burden of unemployment and urged the provision of work by national and local authorities. In November 1921 a deputation from the Southampton Guardians requested

1 *Hampshire Independent*, 18 December 1920

2 Southampton Board of Guardians, Minute Book, 1918-19: Southampton RO, SC/AG1/3/14.

Council works for the 6000 currently on out-relief. Political considerations reinforced financial incentives when in January 1922 the Independent majority on Council denounced the liberal relief scale operated by the controlling Labour element on the Board.[1] The reduction of maximum out-relief under the pressure of the Ministry of Health's refusal to sanction the extension of the Board's overdraft,[2] Council criticisms and electoral considerations, gave added urgency to efforts to promote relief works as a means of reflecting, and hopefully deflecting, the strong (and occasionally violent) representations of ex-servicemen's associations, trade unions and the nascent organisations of the unemployed themselves. Though party conflict was eliminated by the electoral reduction of Labour representation on the Board from 10 to 3, the enduring desire to minimise the poor rate was apparent in the proposal of the new Independent majority for a civic conference to consider relief works.

The most persistent pressure for relief work came from trade unions,[3] generally through the medium of the Trades Council which in July 1921 despatched the first of a series of deputations on behalf of 12,000 unemployed. One member of this deputation declared, 'he was afraid that, unless the Councils of the country in general, and the government in particular, were prepared to do something, and that very shortly, the men who were told they were returning to a country fit for heroes would see that the country was reserved for heroes only'.[4] Despite indignation at the threatening language, Council acceded unanimously to the deputation's request for a Special Committee to consider a substantial list of relief works.

The apparent success of this militant stance was both a reflection of and a further stimulus to the inability of the Trades Council to contain the protests of the unemployed, who were represented at the Special Committee in September 1921 by a newly-formed Official Committee of the Unemployed. In April 1922 a similarly-titled body claimed before the Southampton Guardians that the unions were doing nothing for their unemployed members.[5] The initiative in terms of protest, if not necessarily of effective pressure, was passing from the moderate Trades Council to a more aggressive local branch of the Communist-led National Unemployed Workers' Movement.

1 *Hampshire Independent*, 20 January 1922.

2 *Hampshire Independent*, 20 January 1922. The Board's overdraft had risen to £31,673. The maximum out-relief allowable to a family was reduced from £3 to £2 13s shortly prior to the Guardians' elections.

3 Especially the local branches of the Transport and General Workers Union, the Ironfounders and the National Association of Operative House and Ship Painters and Decorators.

4 County Borough of Southampton, *Minutes of Proceedings of Council and Committees, 1920-21*, p. 893.

5 *Hampshire Independent*, 21 April 1922.

Despite the evident dissatisfaction of the protagonists of works with progress by the autumn of 1921, Southampton Council had not been entirely unsympathetic. Relief works within the remit of the Council fell into two distinct categories: those of a minor nature capable of being financed out of annual revenue and more substantial works requiring the loan sanction of the Ministry of Health and eligible for grant aid from the Ministry of Transport or Unemployment Grants Committee. In the former category action was initially inhibited by the opposition of the General Purposes Committee on the grounds of distortion of the labour market by Out-of-Work Donations and the high cost and short supply of materials.[1] In February 1921, however, a minor road improvement was advanced as a relief measure. Council Committees also responded sympathetically to representations from the painters' union, whose secretary was a Labour Councillor and effective lobbyist.[2] The mass of the unemployed were, however, dependent on the promotion of more substantial schemes. Beginning in November 1920, Southampton Council had prior to the Special Meeting in September 1921 submitted schemes to the value of £204,000 for loan sanction and unemployment relief grants. Though £82,000 worth were rejected as not likely to employ sufficient unskilled labour, grant aid was approved for schemes costed at £113,000. Yet tenders had been accepted only to the value of £58,000.[3] In March 1921 the press had reported the first men - 12 of them - at work on a relief scheme.[4]

The Special Committee, meeting a few weeks before municipal elections, recommended minor projects on school repairs and recreation grounds together with major road, drainage and tramway works to be submitted for loan sanctions to the value of £99,000.[5] Since the two largest projects, jointly worth £56,000, had already received grant approval without being put to tender, this figure incorporated as much public relations as real substance.

In October 1921 it was claimed that relief works would provide employment for 10 per cent of those idle[6] yet in December there were only 86 employed on Council relief works, against a live register of 10,055.[7] While these figures illuminate the very limited impact of

1 *Hampshire Independent*, 24 May 1919.

2 Interview with Sir James Matthews, secretary to Southampton Labour Group from 1929, on 16 July 1974. Their union claimed 200 unemployed painters in early 1921. The enduring tendency to a high rate of unemployment among ship painters is stressed in Geoffrey R Denton, *A report on unemployment in the ship-building and ship-repairing industry of Southampton* (Southampton County Borough Council, 1961) pp. 15-17.

3 *Minutes of Proceedings of Council and Committees, 1920-21*.

4 *Hampshire Advertiser*, 11 March 1921.

5 *Hampshire Advertiser*, 8 October 1921; *Minutes of Proceedings of Council and Committees, 1920-21*, p. 997.

6 *Hampshire Advertiser*, 8 October 1921.

7 *Hampshire Advertiser*, 17 December 1921.

works specifically designed for relief purposes, they take no account of employment generated on work ineligible for relief grants. In October 1921, for instance, a tramways extension project undertaken without grant aid was employing 140 men recruited through the British Legion, Board of Guardians and Employment Exchange.[1] Total employment on Council works was determined by total municipal expenditure, in particular on capital account, much of which, though dependent on loan sanction or even in receipt of central grants as with housing, was ineligible for the higher rates of grant for works advanced on account of unemployment. Conversely it is evident from the statements of Council officers that some schemes receiving grant aid as relief projects were at least equally motivated by the desire to obtain a subsidy towards essential work deferred by the war. UGC aid was received for one scheme initially formulated because the state of the roads had necessitated the suspension of an omnibus service after only one month's operation.[2]

Thus even in the depths of the post-war slump the efforts of government to mitigate unemployment through a specifically tailored grants system were at best tangentially related to the local initiatives on which they were dependent. Relief works were defined by eligibility for grant as much as vice-versa. Though total capital expenditure rose substantially from 1918 to 1921,[3] it was the very limited scale of designated relief works in the face of soaring unemployment which led the *Hampshire Advertiser* to comment that 'much had been promised, but little had been done'[4] and a Labour Guardian to suggest that on the Council there had been too much talk and not enough work.[5] Council officers blamed government procrastination.[6] In view of the submission of schemes with low labour content, the low proportion of approved grants leading to early requests for tenders, conflicts between Council Committees regarding their respective share of the costs and complications arising from party political considerations outside the unemployment issue, Council could hardly claim for itself the maximum expedition, its determination perhaps being blunted by the general optimism for the future voiced by civic leaders and local press,[7] despite present indicators.

Independent leaders' criticisms of central administration received some support from the Local Employment Committee.[8] Though Labour leaders insisted that government responsibilities did not

1 *Minutes of Proceedings of Council and Committees, 1920-21*, p. 1125.

2 *Hampshire Advertiser*, 7 January 1921; *Minutes of Proceedings of Council and Committees, 1920-21*, p. 315.

3 See Appendix 2, Tables N - Q.

4 *Hampshire Advertiser*, 31 December 1921.

5 *Hampshire Advertiser*, 29 October 1921.

6 *Hampshire Advertiser*, 18 February 1921.

7 Eg *Hampshire Independent*, 29 September 1922; *Southampton Chamber of Commerce, Annual Report, 1922-23*, p. 23.

8 *Minutes of Proceedings of Council and Committees, 1920-21*, p. 1009.

exonerate the Council, they too were by late 1921 convinced that little could be done without a change in government policies.[1] Discontent was in part the product of local resentment of the whole basis of government policy in shifting the major share of the burden of relief work onto local authorities, in part of the restrictive conditions under which grants were offered, but predominantly of government inconsistency in on the one hand encouraging local authority expenditure on relief works while on the other hand urging the restriction of general capital expenditure under an increasingly vigorous retrenchment campaign associated with the redemption of the National Debt and the inauguration of deflation as a prelude to the restoration of the Gold Standard. As early as August 1919 Admiralty economies had resulted in lay-offs at Southampton's principal shipyard. By mid-1921 the appeals of the UGC were counteracted by pressure from the Ministry of Health for the reduction of local authority capital expenditure and by the curtailment of housing subsidies, reinforced by the 'Geddes Axe' emanating from the Report of the Committee on National Expenditure in December 1921. For Council's spending committees, Whitehall urgings were given added weight by prevailing 7½ per cent interest rates and by a sharp increase in the borough rate for 1920-1.[2] The deferring of work as an economy measure began in March 1921. Finance Committee vetting of all new capital expenditure was supplemented early in 1922 by the implementation of wage and salary cuts for municipal employees. Requests for relief work now generally met with a negative response. Though the full impact of economy was not evident on capital account until the financial year 1923-4, from the autumn of 1921 it offset employment deriving from relief works.

The contradictions in local policy in the post-war slump, though reflecting the national scene, had equally strong roots within the borough, finding expression in party political conflict. In a Council debate in March 1921, Independent leader Alderman Kimber placed the responsibility for persistent unemployment on the trade unions, and in particular the current joiners' strike, while Labour leader Councillor Lewis accused the Independents of 'economy stunts'.[3] Though in September 1921 Independents and Labour voted together in favour of higher rates of grant, rejecting the proposals of the Cabinet Committee on Unemployment for the transfer of an increased share of the financial burden to local authorities, a Labour resolution urging Parliament to adopt a national policy with the necessary finances was rejected by 23 votes to 19 in favour of an appreciation of 'the efforts which the government is taking to restore our national trade'.[4]

1 *Hampshire Advertiser*, 4 March 1921.

2 For rate statistics see Appendix 2, Tables J and K. The sharp rise in 1920-21 reflected the costs of the absorption of the Itchen districts, the high level of capital expenditure (Appendix 2, Table M) and the rising burden of poor-relief expenditure.

3 *Hampshire Advertiser*, 4 March 1921. The strike over wage-reductions, which lasted eight months, was estimated to have cost 600 jobs and over £1 million in lost wages (*Hampshire Advertiser*, 20 August 1921; 10 September 1921).

4 *Hampshire Advertiser*, 1 October 1921; *Minutes of Proceedings of Council and Committees, 1920-21*, pp. 997-9.

The local strength of the economy campaign was an inevitable product of the nature of the dominant Independent party with its origins in demands for economic administration in the interests of the ratepayers.[1] The *Hampshire Advertiser* now argued that 'the Ratepayers have precious little to spare for speculative altruism - the best thing is to let the problem be solved, if it can be solved, in the ordinary course of reviving operations in the industrial and commercial world'[2] - a view endorsed by the borough's Ratepayers' Association, supplemented from April 1921 by the efforts of the Municipal Vigilance Committee of the local Middle Classes Union to oppose inessential expenditure and extravagance by Council and Guardians.[3] Most consistent among the advocates of economy, in the interests of reducing the tax and rate burden on industry, was the Chamber of Commerce, well represented among Independent councillors.[4] Though a minority of Independents displayed an enduring sympathy for relief works, the conflict between economy and unemployment relief was increasingly polarised along party lines. If Labour's electoral gains in 1919 had helped stimulate the discussion of relief works, Independent successes in 1921 and 1922 apparently justified the emphasis on economy and rate reduction.

For Labour it was axiomatic, in the words of one Councillor, that 'one cannot cure unemployment and cry economy in the same breath'.[5] Though Southampton's Trades Council and Labour Representation Committee was united on the principle of relief works, their implementation presented practical political difficulties. As their secretary expressed the position: 'while the Trades Council placed no obstacle in the way of work schemes, they would oppose the exploitation of the unemployed or the breaking down of Trade Union conditions'.[6] This reservation contrasted with the belief of the Chamber of Commerce that 'in view of the impossibility of levying further taxation, and in order

1 The *Hampshire Independent* on 20 October 1922 commented that economy was the sole unifying factor in the Independent Party.

2 *Hampshire Advertiser*, 23 July 1921. One ward Ratepayers' Association rejected the Chairman of the Electricity Committee, a former Liberal, as its candidate on account of 'too expensive policies'. Other Ratepayers' Associations denounced the rating reassessment as 'exhorbitant'.

3 Between its inception in 1919 and mid-1921 the local branches of the Middle Classes Union (later re-named the National Citizens Union) recruited some 2200 members, including a number of Councillors and Guardians (*Hampshire Advertiser*, 14 April 1921). Following claims of success in securing seats for 'progressive' candidates in the Guardians' elections in 1922, the Union disbanded its ward associations, fading from the scene after 1923.

4 For instance, in 1925 the Chamber passed a resolution urging that, 'the sternest possible economy must be practised by the state. No possible opportunity must be neglected of reducing taxation' (*Annual Report of Southampton Chamber of Commerce, 1925-26*, p. 10).

5 *Hampshire Advertiser*, 4 March 1921.

6 *Hampshire Advertiser*, 1 October 1921.

that funds available should . . . afford relief to the largest number of the unemployed, it should be an instruction to the Authorities . . . that it is not incumbent upon them to pay the present Trade Union rate of wages under employment schemes, but rather a reasonable rate of remuneration with the object of . . . not offering attractions to men to leave other jobs'.[1] A Ministry of Labour recommendation in 1922 of a maximum for relief work of 75 per cent of the local authority wage clashed with trade union pressure for a fair wages clause in all Council contracts. The same principle underlay Labour opposition to the Southampton Guardians' offer of a sum equal to the savings in out-relief (fixed by the Ministry of Health at a maximum of 75 per cent of the average local wage) in return for Council-sponsored work schemes.[2] The Trades Council also opposed a housing scheme designed to employ ex-servicemen on the grounds of dilution,[3] while political considerations led the Labour Group to adopt an at best ambivalent stance on a number of projects capable of generating substantial employment.[4]

By the autumn of 1921 relief works had been nipped in the bud by the national economy campaign, coinciding locally with the growing articulation of the Ratepayer interest and the backlash from the joiners' strike. Nevertheless, the supplications and strictures of Guardians, British Legion, Trades Council and others continued unabated and even in 1922 and 1923 a select number of modest relief schemes were promoted. By 1924 the accomplishment of a substantial rate reduction, combined with the reinvigoration of the UGC by the first Labour government, led to the formulation of the two largest relief schemes to date, for water-main and sewerage works jointly estimated at £209,000. Though employment on these schemes lasted until 1927, the return of a Conservative government in 1925 followed by a new Economy Act and the restriction of UGC aid to areas with unemployment above 10 per cent of the insured workforce eliminated the possibility of further grant-aided schemes in Southampton. New relief works, which now had to be borne entirely on the rates, were henceforth few and small, consisting largely of painting works. Though Labour's Parliamentary candidates protested at the government's virtual abolition of relief works and both Borough and Trades Council condemned Churchill's raids on the Road Fund, the majority of Independents, comforted by the belated decline in the live register, apparently endorsed the belief of the borough's senior Conservative MP, Edwin Perkins, that 'it was for everyone to keep a stiff upper lip and effect economy in every way'.[5]

1 Minutes of a meeting of the Board of Directors of Southampton Chamber of Commerce held on 22 March 1921. The Minute books are in the possession of the Southampton Chamber of Commerce.

2 *Hampshire Independent*, 23 June 1922.

3 *Hampshire Advertiser*, 17 June 1921.

4 These included the rebuilding of Taunton's Endowed School, a major docks extension scheme, the construction of the Civic Centre, an extension to Pirelli's Cable Works and the sale of land to the Ford Motor Company for the erection of their principal United Kingdom plant.

5 *Southern Daily Echo*, 15 April 1926.

The relative ease with which orthodox advocates of economy attained the dominant influence was in part due to the tenuous theoretical basis of the case for works in the 1920s, resting in the absence of 'Keynesian' concepts of deficient demand and multiplier theory on essentially ethical foundations. The Labour Group, unions and the unemployed themselves, locally bereft even of underconsumptionist theories, proclaimed as an article of faith from the late nineteenth century the 'right to work' in preference to maintenance. Non-Labour Guardians and their allies asserted an equally traditional belief in the 'duty to work' in return for maintenance, expressed in Edwin Perkin's view that 'we cannot allow our fellow citizens to starve in the streets because there are no jobs for them, but we should get something in return for the help the country gives them'[1] - an argument bearing more relation to poor-law test work than to fully-fledged public works. Nor did practical experience even of grant-aided works offer much to convince the sceptics. Administrative complications were daunting, UGC conditions alone being varied in each of ten circulars between 1921 and 1924. Conditions respecting the recruitment of labour, according to the Borough Engineer, 'have caused loss of money and time, and irritation to all concerned',[2] while Council committees resented the insistence from mid-1923 on the use of British materials irrespective of costs. Even after grant aid and loan sanctions had been received, schemes were impeded by shortage of materials and even, ironically, of skilled workmen.[3] Accurate estimation of costs proved virtually impossible and the UGC was by no means invariably prepared to sanction excess expenditure for grant purposes. Deadlines for commencement and completion were generally unrealistic, especially where land purchase was necessary.[4] Uncertainty as to the likely state of employment at the probable date of commencement was therefore an added disincentive to the 'advancement' of work.

Work appropriate to the unskilled majority was not necessarily suited to ex-servicemen, some of them incapable of heavy labour, or to skilled men, strongly represented by their unions, and non-manuals. On average only about half the expenditure on relief schemes fell to wage costs. Though the incomplete nature of surviving documentation prohibits the accurate calculation of the impact of relief schemes in Southampton in terms of cost effectiveness or the level of unemployment, evidence derived from a selective number of Southampton schemes approved by the UGC suggests a cost per man-week of direct labour of £12 4s.[5] Even allowing for grant aid averaging 35 per cent of total

1 *Hampshire Independent*, 27 October 1922.

2 Southampton RO, SCT/135. Special exception was taken to the regulation excluding for grant purposes the wages of permanent Council employees even when necessary in a supervisory role or for the provision of special skills. For details of changing grant terms, see *Final Report of the Unemployment Grants Committee*, *BPP*, 1932-33, Cmd. 4353, xv.

3 Especially bricklayers (*Hampshire Advertiser*, 7 January 1921; *Southern Daily Echo*, 26 February 1926).

4 One scheme approved in October 1924 was not actually commenced until February 1926.

5 Calculated from statistics in a sample of registers of schemes submitted to the Unemployment Grants Committee, retained in PRO LAB 4/244-9.

costs and the generation of an equal volume of indirect employment - the UGC's own estimate - the cost to the local authority at £4 per man-week was still distinctly higher than (nationally financed) unemployment insurance benefits, maximum Southampton out-relief for a family at £3 a week or the wages of unskilled Corporation employees at £2 19s a week before economy cuts.[1] In the absence of any multiplier concept, and given the preference for economy over expenditure on the part of the Independent majority, there was every apparent justification for the belief that maintenance costs were distinctly cheaper than the provision of work.

In 1926, the peak year for actual expenditure on relief works in the 1920s, the anticipated employment, calculated from the limited evidence available, was probably equivalent to 3.6 per cent of a live register approximately half that of the peak of local unemployment in 1921.[2] It seems safe to conclude that in Southampton in the 1920s the contribution of relief works to the reduction of unemployment was never greater than, and generally far less than, this figure. As the Labour Group stated as early as October 1921, 'Unemployment is a national problem which cannot be solved by local effort',[3] because in the words of a joint Trades Union/Independent Labour Party resolution, 'of the inadequacy for the task of the powers and resources of local authorities'.[4] For others the conclusion to be drawn from local experience was not that public (as opposed to relief) works had not been properly tried but that having been tried they had once again proved ineffective, their enduring if intermittent advocacy being a recognition of political rather than economic realities.

V

During the doldrums from 1925 to 1929, the widely-held conviction that unemployment was a national issue in which local initiatives had proved ineffficacious was evident in the low profile presented by the unemployment question in Southampton. Changing popular attributions

1 *Minutes of Proceedings of Council and Committees, 1920-21*, p. 68. A 10 per cent economy cut was imposed in two stages during 1921.

2 Calculated from information in PRO LAB 4/245 and from the Southampton live register of the unemployed published in the local press. The utility of the Southampton statistics is seriously impaired by the extent of the assumptions necessary to their formulation from highly selective data (especially their dependence on estimates of potential employment rather than records of actual numbers employed). However, these statistics compare quite closely with those derived from national UGC data by Keith J Hancock, 'The reduction of unemployment as a problem of public policy, 1920-29', *Economic History Review*, 2nd series, XV (1962) 328-43.

3 *Hampshire Advertiser*, 1 October 1921.

4 *Hampshire Advertiser*, 3 November 1923.

of the causes of prolonged unemployment from the war to the General Strike or monetary policy did little to stimulate local initiatives.[1] The reduction in the live register of unemployed in Southampton, though delayed, was ultimately more pronounced than in other ports, stabilising at around 5000. The growth in port activity, accompanied in 1927 by the initiation of a major docks extension scheme, gave substance to expressions of optimism in Southampton's future prospects, while the stabilisation of the rates permitted the expansion of local authority capital expenditure, relief works receiving little more than token advocacy from any quarter until 1928.

In that year, as in 1920, the revivification of relief works was the result of a government initiative, focused once again on the plight of a specific group, the Welsh miners, through the Industrial Transference Scheme designed to facilitate the redistribution of labour from depressed to more prosperous areas. In March 1928 the Ministry of Health invited Southampton's Advisory Committee on Juvenile Employment to provide employment for 100 Welsh boys. Despite fears that the Committee's prestige would be lowered by finding jobs for transferred youths while local adolescents were unemployed, the Committee reported in February 1929 that it was making every effort to obtain the requested vacancies.[2] In September 1928 the Council received a circular letter from the Prime Minister urging assistance for the distressed areas, backed up by generous UGC terms for schemes employing transferred labour. Though fears were again expressed, especially by the Labour Group, for the impact of miners at the end of their period of relief work on the local pool of 4380 unemployed and on the housing shortage, the majority accepted the Borough Engineer's view of the suitability of transferred labour for a number of schemes of 'necessary work which would in other circumstances not be done so quickly'.[3] Loan sanction and grant approval were obtained for road and sewerage schemes to the value of £190,000, conditional on 50 per cent of the anticipated 400 jobs going to transferred men.[4] However, work on the first schemes from June 1929 reinforced doubts as to the merits of transference. Practical difficulties were experienced concerning the level of maintenance and the provision of and payment for accommodation. The Vale of Neath Labour Party,

1 As late as 1929, Captain Cunningham-Reid, prospective Conservative candidate for Southampton, claimed, 'The General Strike was deliberately called to create unemployment, and for that purpose alone' (*Hampshire Advertiser*, 2 February 1929).

2 Southampton RO Acc. 1305: Minute Book of the Itchen Sub-Committee of the Southampton Advisory Committee on Juvenile Employment, minutes of meetings on 12 April 1928 and 11 February 1929.

3 *Minutes of Proceedings of Council and Committees 1928-29*, p. 200; *Hampshire Advertiser*, 2 February 1929. Though Southampton headed the list of provincial towns subscribing to the national Miners' Distress Fund, with £4275 16s 6d, the views of the Labour Group were shared by local ward associations and by the Southampton Trades Council (*Hampshire Advertiser*, 20 October 1928).

4 Southampton RO SCT 134, Boxes 43 and 50; *Hampshire Advertiser*, 20 April, 22 June 1929.

writing to the Southampton Trades Council in January 1930, protested at the standard of accommodation provided and claimed that 200 men had received only a week's work instead of the promised ten months as a result of over-recruitment.[1] The Trades Council replied that though nine-tenths of the complaints were untrue, the Southampton Labour Group had opposed transference from the outset due to the need to protect their own people. In May 1927 Council rejected a Ministry of Labour proposal to establish a retraining centre under the transference scheme in Southampton itself.[2] By June 1930, with local unemployment once again soaring, Council was declaring its preference for relief works without commitment to transferred labour, at the price of foregoing the higher rates of grant.[3] The majority of subsequent works incorporated a requirement for the employment of 80 per cent local labour. The number of completed removals into Southampton under the transference scheme fell from 27 in 1929 to 10 in 1930 and 1 in 1931[4] by which date the *Hampshire Advertiser* was expressing the local consensus in stating that 'the port has a great future, but at present it has all the unskilled labour it can cope with'.[5]

VI

Despite second thoughts over transference, relief works in general were given added impetus in the 1929 general election. Though the greatest emphasis came from Liberal endorsement of Lloyd George's programme, the victorious Labour candidates also stressed the national responsibility for relieving the rate burden of unemployment through development schemes.[6] With the incentive of the Labour Government's

1 Southampton RO D/TU, Minute Book of Southampton Trades Council, meeting on 8 January 1930; *Hampshire Advertiser*, 11 January 1930.

2 *Hampshire Advertiser*, 18 May 1929. A centre was eventually opened in October 1935.

3 *Minutes of Proceedings of Council and Committees, 1929-30*, p. 876. While the Public Assistance Committee reacted to complaints against the importation of labour by outside contractors by advocating local contracts irrespective of the lowest tender, with an 80 per cent local labour clause, the Electricity Committee rejected such a clause, insisting on the lowest tender.

4 Minutes of Evidence of the Ministry of Labour to *The Royal Commission on the Geographical Distribution of the Industrial Population*, Non-Parliamentary Papers 1938, Appendix IV, Table xi, p. 329.

5 *Hampshire Advertiser*, 20 June 1931.

6 *Hampshire Advertiser*, 4, 11, 18, 25 May 1929. Labour candidates also recommended as remedies for unemployment a 48-hour week and the raising of the school leaving age. Conservative candidates ridiculed Lloyd George's proposals as a mere palliative, stressing the merits of derating and advocating 'safeguarding' measures, together with strict economy in the interests of reducing the rate burden on industry.

improved grant terms from the autumn of 1929, Southampton Council supplemented its transference schemes with proposals for a Five Year Road Programme, the construction of a Civic Centre and water and sewerage works, totalling £1,100,000, together with a three year education building programme and the acceleration of house building and slum clearance.[1] A Town Meeting in July 1930 endorsed further projects including a civic aerodrome. In addition, the Harbour Board received grant aid for a £11,000 scheme for improvements to the Town Quay. Though a £700,000 harbour improvement was rejected for grant purposes owing to the speculative nature and low employment potential of dredging works, a limited scheme was advanced without grant aid on favourable terms offered by the dredging company to keep men and machines in work.[2]

By 1931 the policy of countering unemployment through grant-aided works was again in conflict with renewed calls for national economy in response to the deepening financial crisis in the wake of international depression, coming to a head, as a decade earlier, with the report of a Committee on National Expenditure in July 1931. Though it was the May Committee's recommendations on unemployment insurance which prompted the collapse of the Labour government, its strictures on the grants system led to reduced grant terms in September 1931 and the cessation of the acceptance of new schemes in January 1932.[3]

The works schemes of the early 1930s exhibited similar difficulties to those of the 1920s. Terms of grant were subject to frequent amendment under a system of added complexity. UGC deadlines necessitated the drafting of one major scheme in a day and a half. Frequent haggling arose over commencement and completion dates, while overspending was endemic as 'the time available was all too short to give all the consideration necessary to a scheme of this magnitude'.[4]

1 Southampton RO SCT 134, Boxes 43 and 50; SCT 135; TC Box 21. Also, *Minutes of Proceedings of Council and Committees*, 1929-30.

2 PRO BT 56/33 and MT 48/20. *Hampshire Advertiser*, 28 September 1929 and 25 January 1930.

3 Southampton was already experiencing the impact of reduced military expenditure, affecting particularly the principal shipyard, John I Thorneycroft Ltd. Employment in Southampton was also affected by the cancellation of a £1 million government contract for Supermarine flying boats (*Hampshire Advertiser*, 23 January 1932).

4 Southampton RO SCT 134, Box 43. The increasingly frequent rejection of excess expenditure for grant purposes led the Town Clerk to write to the Ministry of Transport in 1933: 'I think the Ministry will agree that the real reason for declining to accede to the Corporation's application for grant towards the excess expenditure [on the Five-Year Road Programme] was the policy of cutting down expenditure to the greatest possible extent owing to the financial crisis which developed in the late summer of 1931' (Southampton RO, TC Box 21).

Employment potential on the other-hand was frequently over-estimated. On one scheme the actual employment of less than half the anticipated numbers was explained by the use of additional mechanical equipment.[1] Though information is again incomplete, while relief schemes in the early 1930s were more efficient than those of the 1920s, they were unlikely even at their peak to have generated direct employment equivalent to more than 5 per cent of the live register at an average cost of something over £7 per man week.[2]

Until the spring of 1931 the economy lobby in Southampton was effectively held in balance by the proponents of works. In March 1931 Independent calls for economy were given focus in a Council debate which was virtually a replay of exactly a decade earlier, Alderman Kimber criticising Works and Education as 'spending committees' while Alderman Lewis dismissed 'Tory economy stunts' as 'eyewash' when there was £47,000 carried forward unspent from schemes budgeted for 1930.[3] By the autumn, the Chamber of Commerce, its influence enhanced by the unique decision of the Corporation to become a subscribing member, was strongly deprecating the encouragement of unnecessary local expenditure through the grants system, drawing attention to the increase in Southampton's loan debt per capita from £13 12s 5d in 1923 to £24 15s 4d in 1930.[4] Local opinion was further polarised by the opposition of Southampton's Labour MPs to Ramsay Macdonald's leadership of the National Government and intensified by the impending combination of municipal and general elections, in both of which Labour suffered substantial reverses. The implementation of economy measures in Southampton from September 1931, amplified by apparent electoral endorsement, included the abandonment or deferral of works costed at £660,000,[5] including the halting of work on the Civic Centre due to Ministry of Health refusal to sanction the third block owing to heavy excess expenditure to date.[6] An Economy Sub-Committee was to vet all future capital expenditure and consider wage and salary reductions. By the increase of budget surpluses from an average of £3000 a year between 1927 and 1931 to £98,000 between 1931 and 1934 and £132,000

1 Southampton RO SCT 134 Box 50.

2 Calculated from data in Southampton RO and in the local press. For reservations regarding the highly selective nature of the surviving data, see footnote 2, page 76.

3 *Hampshire Advertiser*, 21 March 1930.

4 *Hampshire Advertiser*, 6 September, 6 December 1930; Minute Book of Southampton Chamber of Commerce, General Meeting on 1 October 1931.

5 *Hampshire Advertiser*, 12 December 1931; 26 March 1932. Economy measures included a review of the education building programme and the deferment of a substantial part of the road programme as well as water-main and sewerage works.

6 *Hampshire Advertiser*, 12 December 1931; 16 July 1932. The construction of the Civic Centre was currently employing 300 men.

in the financial year 1934-5, municipal capital expenditure was reduced by two-thirds between 1931 and 1934.[1]

Though the dismantling of the grants system had eliminated the principal financial incentive for local authority relief works, their implementation continued to be advocated by Labour Group, Trades Council and Unemployed Workers' Movement. The increasing influence of the latter, with a 6000 strong deputation to Council in October 1932, an Unemployed Petition and Demonstration Committee with 2350 signatures in October 1933 and a deputation in October 1934 which acrimoniously attacked Labour councillors for hiding behind standing orders,[2] was the source of much embarrassment for Trades Council and Labour Group acting in accordance with TUC instructions in refusing to recognise the Communist-led organisation. Their tactical concentration in the autumn prelude to municipal elections and the seasonal unemployment peak secured the appointment of a Special Council Committee on Unemployment in 1932, though two Unemployed Workers' Movement Candidates, standing in the 1934 municipal elections for the first time, secured only 69 votes between them. A more sympathetic response was given to renewed pressure from ex-service organisations, experiencing a resurgence in membership.[3] In December 1932, with the live register at a record 15,526, the Chairman of a reconstituted Local Employment Committee issued the first of a new series of appeals to householders and employers to spread employment and encourage local trade by bringing forward repairs.[4] Council's own Public Assistance Committee inherited in April 1930, along with the Guardians' maintenance responsibilities, some of their predilections, arguing that unemployment suffered by Southampton as a port should be a national charge and urging works schemes to maintain maximum entitlement to insurance benefits and thus keep down public assistance expenditure.[5]

In part the resilience of the case for works in the face of the limited impact of schemes inaugurated, renewed calls for economy and the abolition of grants was a product of more sophisticated economic

1 *Hampshire Advertiser*, 21 February 1934.

2 *Hampshire Advertiser*, 22 October 1931; 21 October 1933; 20 October, 22 December 1934. For relations between the Unemployed Workers' Movement and the Trades Council, see the latter's Minute Books (Southampton RO D/TU).

3 The Shirley branch of the British Legion grew from 20 to 130 members in a year (*Hampshire Advertiser*, 15 October 1932).

4 *Hampshire Advertiser*, 3 December 1932. Apart from the Southern Railway Company (see section VII), only the Southampton Gas Company seems to have responded, clearing the site for a new gasholder in order to generate employment (*Southern Daily Echo*, 17 February 1933).

5 Eg *Hampshire Advertiser*, 20 May 1933. The Public Assistance Committee utilised its own limited potential to generate work and in addition exhibited a distinctly more favourable response than the Parliamentary and General Purposes Committee to resolutions from other Councils advocating works. The attitude of the Assistance Committee was possibly also influenced by conflict with the Ministry of Health over Southampton's Transitional Payments scale.

arguments. In announcing Labour's conversion to the Civic Centre project in 1928, Lewis had emphasised the beneficial effects of the steady flow of wages, 'not only to the work-people concerned but also to a large number of trades-people as well who supply the workers with their necessities'.[1] In 1931 the Labour Group secretary argued that the reduction of expenditure to balance the budget would destroy industrial confidence, increase unemployment and lead through increased public assistance to higher rates.[2] Labour stress on the need to raise the level of purchasing power received some Independent support. The Chairman of the Education Committee, quoting Keynes' epigram on the saving of 5s putting a man out of work for a day, stated his own view that 'part of the depression . . . at the present time is due to the reluctance to spend on the part of people who have money to spend'.[3] Though the majority of Independents went with the tide of economy in the autumn of 1931, by January 1933 one Independent alderman was prepared to admit, 'I think our corporation went economy mad a few months ago. I believe the policy today should be wise spending'.[4] Similar views were expressed by the borough's Conservative MP, William Craven-Ellis.[5] The fundamental concept of at least a first-stage multiplier had by the early 1930s become fairly common currency among the advocates of relief works, though at no point was deficit financing, and therefore public works in the full Keynesian sense, advocated in Southampton.[6]

1 *Hampshire Advertiser*, 20 October 1928.

2 *Hampshire Advertiser*, 19 September 1931.

3 *Hampshire Advertiser*, 24 January 1931. The *Advertiser* itself commented that, 'True economy should not be confused with hoarding, which at a time like this is "sinful"'.

4 *Southern Daily Echo*, 19 January 1933.

5 Eg *Hampshire Advertiser*, 30 January 1932. In a book, *The rebuilding of Britain* (Allen & Unwin, 1935), Craven-Ellis advocated the use of local authority loans and building society funds to generate employment through a national slum clearance and rebuilding programme. His fellow Southampton MP, National Liberal Sir Charles Barrie, remained critical of inessential expenditure on such items as road schemes.

6 Cf the national picture discussed in Donald I Mackay, David J C Forsyth and David M Kelly, 'The discussion of public works programmes, 1917-35: some remarks on the Labour Movement's contribution', *International Review of Social History*, XI (1966) 8-17. In fact more pervasive in Southampton than diluted Keynesism, was the economics of 'Social Credit' whose local branch, founded in 1932, included prominent businessmen and the Town Clerk and whose views were endorsed in 1933 by an 'Economic Crisis' report by the Chamber of Commerce. Though Social Credit did not advocate public works, it did share with Keynes a belief in deficient demand as the root cause of world depression and an opposition to othodox monetary policy, shared by both Labour MP Ralph Morley and Conservative MP William Craven-Ellis, which no doubt helped to undermine the faith of the local establishment in economy as a nostrum.

In addition to a more sophisticated climate of economic debate, the ethical dimension of the case for work was reinforced by a growing awareness of the social implications of prolonged unemployment. In November 1932 the mayor stated that while a local authority could do little to permanently cure unemployment the causes of which were world-wide, it was nevertheless the duty of municipalities to mitigate 'the evil effects of enforced idleness' on body and mind and thus assist ultimate re-employment.[1] In the spring of 1933 the Methodist churches of Southampton and Portsmouth urged immediate work in view of 'the severe mental, physical and moral deterioration resulting from continued unemployment'.[2] These concerns were reinforced by the report of the borough's Medical Officer of Health for 1933, attributing a marked rise in infantile mortality in two of the poorer wards to unemployment.[3] In the same year a study of poverty in Southampton showed one fifth of the working class below a poverty line defined in relation to wartime rationing, with 65 per cent of local poverty due to unemployment.[4] A sharp rise in the number of juvenile offenders in 1934 was in part attributed to the same cause.[5]

In autumn 1932 a Council Committee, appointed to organise winter relief works in response to a militant deputation of the unemployed, authorised £15,000 worth of work out of revenue and advocated a deputation to the Ministry of Health to seek £195,000 worth of loan sanctions for the restoration of schemes abandoned a year earlier.[6] All work except for key men was to be restricted to those on the local electoral register, with preference given to those close to exhausting their insurance entitlement (and thus likely to become a burden on public assistance). By the turn of the year, 'revenue' schemes had been initiated, the Tramways Committee setting men to work in rotating batches to maximise insurance entitlements.[7] However the mayor, returning from the deputation for loan sanctions, reported the view of the Ministry of Health that 'the relief of unemployment cannot be accepted as a reason for undertaking local government capital expenditure, because it is a much too expensive method of relieving unemployment, having regard to the general financial position of the country'. Indicating the dependence of Council proposals on pressure rather than conviction, the mayor added his own belief that government opposition to works which would add to the rates was 'perfectly sound though it

1 *Hampshire Advertiser*, 12 November 1932.

2 *Minutes of Proceedings of Council and Committees, 1932-33*, pp. 902, 1047.

3 *Annual Report on the Health of the County Borough of Southampton and the Port of Southampton for the year 1933*, p. 4.

4 *Hampshire Advertiser*, 20 May 1933, citing the findings of Percy Ford subsequently published in *Work and wealth in a modern port*, especially Chapter V.

5 Southampton RO DZ 74 (Acc. 332), Southampton Labour Party Speakers' Notes for 1934.

6 *Minutes of Proceedings of Council and Committees, 1931-32*, pp. 1616-18 and 1639-40. The recommendations of the Special Committee were subsequently endorsed by a conference of employers and unions chaired by the mayor (*Hampshire Advertiser*, 26 November 1932).

7 *Minutes of Proceedings of Council and Committees, 1932-33*, p. 201.

may be unwelcome', since given that unemployment was not a temporary evil, the advancement of work must increase future difficulties - a concise reaffirmation of the 'Treasury view'.[1]

This statement prompted in early 1933 a temporary diversion from true public or even relief works through a scheme more reminiscent of nineteenth-century reliance on voluntary effort. Under the Mayor's Welfare Scheme for the Unemployed £8800 was raised in voluntary contributions to provide one or two days work on such tasks as levelling playing fields, for 6000 unemployed volunteers, in return for the supply of boots and clothing, thus avoiding loss of insurance benefits.[2] Though the Welfare Scheme was endorsed by Borough Council, Chamber of Commerce, Rotary, Council of Social Service, Employment Exchange, churches, local press and dignatories, for Labour it was, in the words of Alderman Lewis, 'a ticklish thing to deal with'.[3] It was objected that the work should be done by the Corporation at proper rates of pay, that the scheme involved a means test and smacked of charity. The Trades Council declared the scheme contrary to trade union principles as voluntary labour aggravated the position of both employed and unemployed.[4] Independent accusations of a Labour boycott against a scheme apparently popular with the long-term unemployed persuaded the Labour Group to refrain from outright opposition, though urging the need for genuine works, not doles.

Late in 1933 the Ministry of Health relaxed its resistance to loan sanctions, beginning with the removal of its veto on the Civic Centre, conditional on 'a systematic and considered budgeting for capital expenditure'.[5] The advent of a less economy-conscious mayor[6] facilitated the restoration of suspended road and drainage schemes, the promotion of a Sports Centre and the acceleration of slum clearance, though at no point in the late 1930s did capital expenditure exceed the level of 1930-1. As in the 1920s the revival in expenditure was dependent on rate reduction, achieved in 1934 with the aid of a rating revaluation and accumulated surpluses carried forward. The crucial significance of the rate was now also evident in the ambivalent position of the Labour Group, with at least a theoretical chance of

1 *Hampshire Advertiser*, 3 December 1932.

2 *Southern Daily Echo*, 2 January 1933; *Hampshire Advertiser*, 29 July 1933.

3 *Southern Daily Echo*, 9 February 1933.

4 Southampton RO D/TU. Minute Book of Southampton Trades Council; minutes of meetings of Trades Council on 8 February 1933 and of Executive Committee on 1 March 1933.

5 *Minutes of Proceedings of Council and Committees, 1933-34*, p. 41. The final cost of the Civic Centre at £612,000, compared to an original estimate of £378,000, resulted by 1937 in a rate burden due to excess expenditure equivalent to 0.48 of a penny rate.

6 The economy-conscious Councillor F Woolley was succeeded by the less orthodox Councillor W D Buck, who described the economy campaign as 'a retrograde step from prosperity' (*Hampshire Advertiser*, 30 December 1933).

gaining control of the Council in 1934, criticising the reluctance of Independents to spend while themselves advocating further rate reduction.[1] Despite the ultimate completion of the majority of schemes originally advocated as relief works in 1929 to 1931, the delay imposed by Whitehall had served to re-emphasise the severe political and economic limitations of a local authority as the engine of relief works and in particular the subordination of employment considerations to the rates.

VII

It was evident that in the 1930s as in the 1920s municipal relief works operated well below the level necessary for any significant impact on cyclical as opposed to seasonal unemployment. They were clearly unable to provide an effective substitute for major private contracts, such as an order for six destroyers for the Chilean Navy placed with Southampton's largest shipyard in 1927 giving work for 1000 men for two years.[2] The overhaul of a liner could create 40,000 to 50,000 man-days work, while the cancellation of a sailing cost the jobs of 1000 men.[3] If the local authority lacked the necessary resources, political leverage or unanimity of purpose for a sustained attack on unemployment through public works on this scale, there was in Southampton one body better equipped for the task - the Southern Railway Company as proprietor of the docks and thus the largest single employer in the borough.

In September 1921 the Company revived pre-war plans for an extension of dock facilities. Despite press comment on 'the boon this would be for the unemployed if this task could be commenced at once',[4] its initiation was delayed for five years by indecision on the part of the Company, accentuated by the reluctance of the Borough Council to contribute towards the cost of reclaiming foreshore land and the fears of the Labour Group for the effect on local poverty of the creation of more casual employment.[5] Early in 1927 work commenced on the first stage of the extension, to cost £3 million over four years. By October 1929, 2000 men, a high proportion of them local, were employed on the scheme.[6] The extension of eligibility for unemployment grants under the 1929 Development Act to public utility companies prompted an application for grant aid in order to advance

1 *Hampshire Advertiser*, 24 February 1934.

2 *Southern Daily Echo*, 23 March 1927.

3 *Hampshire Advertiser*, 23 April 1932; *Southern Daily Echo*, 27 February 1935.

4 *Hampshire Advertiser*, 8 October 1921.

5 *Hampshire Advertiser*, 26 November 1921. The Chamber of Commerce, on the other hand, favoured the reclamation scheme, for which the Corporation's share of the costs would be £35,000, as 'of great importance for the expansion of trade and commerce in Southampton', leading to increased employment and rateable value (*Hampshire Independent*, 24 February 1922).

6 *Hampshire Advertiser*, 19 October 1929; 3 March 1933.

the second stage as a contribution towards the reduction of unemployment. At a further cost of £3¼ million, the scheme was the largest project to be submitted to the Development (Public Utility) Advisory Committee. After eight months hard bargaining, attracting the personal attention of J H Thomas as Minister responsible for unemployment, grant terms were agreed and work on the second stage commenced in October 1930, direct employment for 1720 men and indirect employment for 800 being anticipated for five years, with the prospect of increased permanent employment in the area.[1]

The political leverage of the Southern Railway Company was more clearly evident in negotiations, described by J H Thomas as 'very like blackmail', for a grant towards the £1,850,000 construction costs of a new dry dock for Southampton.[2] Here the Company was able to make capital out of the provision of the dock as an essential condition for Cunard's construction of the Queen Mary, a project in which strong government interests were shared by the port of Southampton. The dry dock was claimed to have employed 1000 men over two years from July 1931.[3]

In total, these expansion projects generated direct employment alone for an average of over 2000 men for eight years, equivalent to 20 per cent of the average live register and 23 per cent in the peak year of unemployment in 1932. Undoubtedly the extent and timing of the docks extension was a significant factor in delaying the impact of the Slump on Southampton for at least a year and subsequently in mitigating the effects of reduced municipal expenditure as a retarding influence on economic recovery. Though even this contribution was not without its detractors, the Southampton Guardians attributing the growing number of casuals in their institutions in the late 1920s to the attraction of labour to Southampton as a result of national publicity for the project,[4] on balance the docks extension was clearly in the long- as well as the short-term interests of the borough. In 1931 the Report of the Royal Commission on Transport stated that 'with regard to Southampton we believe its wonderful development has been largely due to the enterprise of the . . . Railway Company',[5] a view endorsed in 1934 by the mayor's attribution of 90 per cent of the

1 PRO MT 48/128. The final grant was equal to 18.3 per cent of the capital cost, compared to the Company's original request for 31.7 per cent and the Ministry's initial offer of 14.3 per cent.

2 PRO MT 48/130. This grant was equal to 28.6 per cent of the capital cost, against an original request for 42.2 per cent.

3 *Hampshire Advertiser*, 27 February 1932. 400 men were also employed for several months on the construction of passenger and cargo sheds. The Southern Railway Company's electrification scheme no doubt also generated some employment for Southampton men in the early 1930s.

4 *Southern Daily Echo*, 21 April 1927. *The Hampshire Advertiser* commented on 30 April 1930, 'What Southampton does not want is a further influx of casual and unskilled labour attracted by press reports of prosperity'. The mayor reacted swiftly to deny reports in the national press in early 1932 that the docks extension might soon absorb all of Southampton's 14,000 unemployed.

5 *Final Report of the Royal Commission on Transport*, *BPP*, 1930-31, Cmd. 3751, xvii, p. 135, paragraph 480.

progress of port and town to the Company's efforts.[1]

VIII

If the docks extension scheme had a significant impact on the pattern of cyclical unemployment, the resultant potential for the expansion of port activities and the associated reclamation of foreshore land available for industrial purposes provided scope for the amelioration of structural deficiencies in the local economy. Despite the advent in the 1920s of vehicle and aircraft manufacture, oil-refining and a tobacco factory, opportunities for a major extension of Pirelli's cable works and the siting of Ford's principal United Kingdom plant in the borough had been lost, in part at least, through insufficient determination on the part of the Council.[2] On the eve of the Slump, the *Hampshire Advertiser*, commenting on the southward drift of industry, declared 'Southampton has reason to look ahead with some complacency'.[3] In 1934 the Rank Company opened the first premises on the reclaimed industrial estate, to be followed by other light consumer industries influenced by Southampton's port facilities and extensive hinterland. While the Corporation paid commendable if exaggerated attention to aviation as a potential counterbalance to the fluctuating fortunes of shipping, in capitalising on the borough's industrial potential they were less energetic. In 1937 MP Craven-Ellis complained that the opening of only 7 new factories and 4 extensions employing a total of 1600 people was a poor performance by comparison to other cities of a similar size.[4] The limitations inherent in Southampton's enduring dependence on the port industries, despite the impact on shipbuilding of rearmament in the late 1930s, remained evident in an intractable minimum of 6000 unemployed.

IX

Despite the consistent advocacy and periodic implementation throughout the inter-war years of works for the relief of Southampton's unemployed, only with the Southern Railway Company's docks extension scheme did the area experience anything approaching fully-fledged counter-depressive public works. Even then, although the scale was sufficient to deflect the trade cycle, the scheme's long-term structural potential was partially allowed to evaporate.

1 *Hampshire Advertiser*, 5 May 1934.

2 Eg *Hampshire Independent*, 22 September 1922. The Corporation was particularly hesitant in taking the necessary Parliamentary powers to enable financial support for a Development Committee in conjunction with the Harbour Board and Chamber of Commerce, or in responding to the Chamber of Commerce's annual plea for the establishment of a Publicity Bureau for the borough.

3 *Hampshire Advertiser*, 28 December 1929. Only 3 weeks earlier, the same paper had quoted the view of Percy Ford, lecturer in economics engaged in a study of Southampton's economy, that though Southampton was growing, it was doing so at a diminishing pace.

4 *Southern Daily Echo*, 22 December 1937.

The promise of a counter-depressive works programme on a national scale contained in the 1909 Development Act was fatally undermined after the first world war by the determination of government to shift a substantial part of the financial burden arising from unprecedented unemployment from national taxes to local rates. The inherent contradiction contained in the grants system's dual requirement that such works should be specifically designed for relief purposes and yet necessary works of public utility in any case tended to render relief grants at best tangential to the determination of the level of municipal expenditure. From the imposition of economy standards on general capital expenditure in 1921, UGC grants served to translate the advancement of work which would not otherwise have been undertaken into the maintenance of works which would otherwise have been abandoned. With the dismantling of the grants system from the autumn of 1931 and the subsequent refusal of loan sanctions, local initiatives were effectively overwhelmed by the regression of national policy beyond even the exhortatory level of the 'Chamberlain circular'.

The evolution of unemployment policy between the wars was thus severely constricted by the necessity of reconciling conflicting national and local interests regarding administrative control, political accountability and financial responsibility. Though local institutions and organisations regularly proclaimed the necessity for a national development programme, this was predominantly motivated by financial considerations arising out of the rate burden of unemployment relief. By the 1930s the traditional ethical case for works was supplemented among local protagonists by renewed emphasis on the social effects of unemployment and by growing economic sophistication. However their grasp of the fundamental principles which would have distinguished public from relief works was at best superficial and inadequate to outweigh the national and municipal impetus of orthodox economy measures. It had been apparent from the early 1920s that local resources, even with grant aid, were quite inadequate for an effective works programme. After 1931 the absence of grant aid re-emphasised for the local authority the financial advantages of maintenance, especially through nationally-funded insurance benefits, rendering the implementation of relief works a matter of political rather than economic considerations. Though the evident difficulty in establishing for any length of time a local consensus regarding relief works reflected national economic and political philosophies, the restraints which they imposed were reinforced by a variety of more localised factors. The time lag in the impact of the trade cycle on Southampton distorted the interplay between national and local responses to economic stimuli. In both 1921 and 1931 local pressure for relief works had barely gathered momentum before becoming stranded on the tide of national economy, though in both cases delayed economic recovery also gave local relief works a degree of second wind. The consistency of local attitudes was further impeded by the subjection of the principle local authority (unlike the Southern Railway Company however) to annual elections which, despite continuity in party administration, accentuated the tendency in national policy for frequent and often sharp changes of emphasis. The coincidence of municipal elections with the winter unemployment peak also exacerbated the emphasis in UGC policy on the relationship between relief works and seasonal unemployment at the expense of increasingly fundamental cyclical and structural problems.

Ultimately institutional inadequacies and ambivalencies in policy reflected the local community itself. For mass unemployment was a social experience which, far from uniting the community against a common enemy, fragmented it between a variety of vested interests, dividing representative and responsible institutions internally and externally and encouraging the evasion of political and financial liability by passing the buck, in the absence of realistic and effective remedies. Certain groups did make some headway. The painters, whose regular requests for work generally received a sympathetic response, were a well-organised pressure group, defined by the skills and seasonality of their trade, associated through building and ship-repairing with industries well represented in local institutions and exercising pressure through public petition and private lobbying in pursuit of limited objectives within the scope of local resources. The Trades Council and Unemployed Workers' Movement, representing the broader interests of the mass of the unemployed, used the blunter tactics of electoral, and even the threat of physical, pressure to achieve occasional concessions, though of a temporary nature and often more in form than substance. Ex-servicemen's organisations combined something of both approaches with a unique degree of public sympathy. The interests of other, less organised groups, such as women and juveniles, were barely considered in relation to relief works.

Against the combined resistance for much of the period of Whitehall, the majority of the Independent Party and the Chamber of Commerce, it is perhaps remarkable that the Labour Group and its allies managed to breath as much life into the case for relief works as it possessed. Labour's influence was, however, constrained by both pragmatic and ideological internal dissentions and by the local electoral system which failed to award political power in proportion to their share of the popular vote.[1] In such circumstances the most influential pressure-group of all was the ratepayers. In a community where even in the depths of the Slump the unemployed were a distinct minority, it was this factor which led to the formation of the Independent Party and subsequently sustained it in office. By the mid-1930s, as the Independents change of name to Ratepayers' Party symbolised, the real dialogue was no longer between the respective merits of works and maintenance but between local rates and national taxes and between expenditure and economy - a dialogue in which, locally as nationally, financial orthodoxy had the loudest voice.

1 Although the Labour Party generally secured a majority of the votes cast in municipal elections in the 1930s, the combination of ward boundaries and tight Independent control of aldermanic seats ensured that they consistently remained a distinct minority on Council (see Appendix 3).

APPENDICES

APPENDIX 1 DISTRIBUTION OF INSURED WORKFORCE, 1923–37

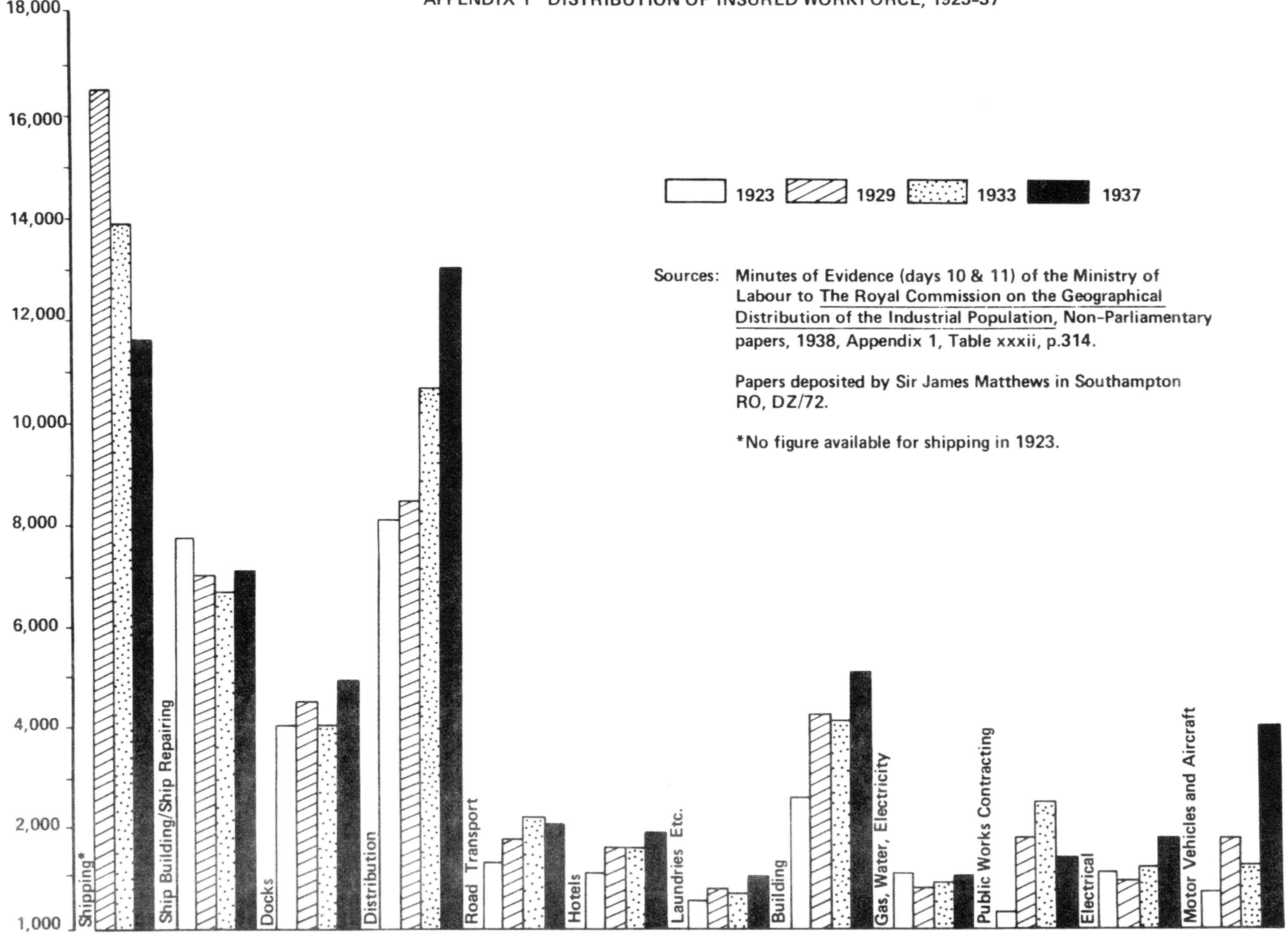

Sources: Minutes of Evidence (days 10 & 11) of the Ministry of Labour to The Royal Commission on the Geographical Distribution of the Industrial Population, Non-Parliamentary papers, 1938, Appendix 1, Table xxxii, p.314.

Papers deposited by Sir James Matthews in Southampton RO, DZ/72.

*No figure available for shipping in 1923.

APPENDIX 2 SOUTHAMPTON, 1919-39: SUMMARY OF ECONOMIC AND SOCIAL STATISTICS

	A	B	C	D	E[a]	F	G	H	I	J[b]
Date	Population	Insured population	Average live register of unemployed	% Unemployed S'oton	% Unemployed UK	Recipients of poor relief on account of unemployment (1 Jan.)	Unemployment relief per ten thousand of population (1 Jan.) S'oton	Unemployment relief per ten thousand of population (1 Jan.) England & Wales	Casuals (1 Jan.)	Poor Rate s d
1919	131,300 [c]	(43,980) [d]	..	..	..	..	..	..	..	2 11½
1920	162,700	.. [d-e]	.. [f-e]	.. [d-e]	3.9	(709) [g]	..	..	8	3 6
1921	161,000	(48,530)	(9,500)	(19.6)	16.9	(950) [g]	..	..	30	4 7¾
1922	163,700	..	(8,300) [f]	..	14.3	4,124	319	196	40	5 3½
1923	165,200	52,450	7,400	14.2	11.7	718	54	189	33	5 7
1924	167,300	..	6,300	11.7	10.3	256 [h]	19 [h]	137	54 [h]	2 10¼ [h]
1925	168,600	..	6,100	11.0	11.3	93	6	84	37	3 6⅛
1926	169,300	57,840	5,700	9.9	12.5	167	10	119	47	3 1¾
1927	169,800	58,330	5,000	8.6	9.7	111	7	141	77	3 4¾
1928	169,900	59,070	4,600	7.8	10.8	112	7	114	47	3 1½
1929	172,300	62,000	5,300	8.6	10.4	41	2	79	55	3 0
1930	175,000	64,390	7,500	11.7	16.1	35	2	62	55	2 6
1931	176,000	62,820	11,100	17.7	21.3	74	4	39	67	2 3
1932	177,500	64,290	13,900	21.6	22.1	168	9	66	85	2 2¼
1933	177,600	63,140	13,000	20.6	19.9	3,691	208	104	149	2 2
1934	177,000	61,000	11,100	18.2	16.7	4,717 [i]	266 [i]	105 [i]	75	2 4¾
1935	177,200	61,270	9,400	15.3	15.5	874	49	112	115	2 7¼
1936	177,400	63,270 [e]	7,200 [e]	11.4 [e]	13.1	723	41	81	91	2 6½
1937	178,700	67,260	6,200	9.2	10.8	375 [i]	21 [i]	59 [i]	76	2 6¾
1938	180,100	70,180	7,100	10.2	12.9	127	7	14	100	2 1¾
1939	181,400	..	5,900	..	10.5	148	8	13	139	2 7

a Comparable in trend but not in absolute level with column D.

b Statistics in these columns apply to the year ending on 31 March of the year shown.

c Including parishes formerly administered by Itchen Urban District Council.

d Bracketed figures are for National Health Insurance, broadly comparable with the scope of Unemployment Insurance after the extention of the latter in November 1920.

e Bars indicate extensions in the scope of Unemployment Insurance.

f Bracketed figures estimated from statistics irregularly printed in the local press.

K[b]	L[b]	M	N[b]	O[b]	P[b]	Q[b]	R	S	
Total rate: S'oton (s d)	Total rate: England & Wales (s d)	Rateable value (1 April) £	Capital expenditure: £	Capital expenditure: Index (1929 prices)	Loans sanctioned: £	Loans sanctioned: Index (1929 prices)	Seamen engaged (1913=100)	Net tons handled (1913=100)	Date
9 5¾	7 8½	659,000	44,000	..	25,000	..	63	25	1919
11 3 c	9 6¾	688,000 c	98,000 c	39 c	255,000 c	111 c	107	59	1920
16 9¼	13 7	809,000 j	496,000[l]	164	763,000	284	130	67	1921
17 3	14 7¼	907,000	809,000	192	774,000	194	182	96	1922
15 7¾	13 1¾	929,000	276,000	59	186,000	44	188	120	1923
11 6¼	12 1¼	964,000	160,000	36	247,000	61	177	124	1924
12 9	11 8¾	1,017,000	293,000	66	406,000	105	195	127	1925
12 2	12 0½	1,046,000	348,000	80	308,000	80	205	131	1926
12 3	12 5	1,076,000	556,000	125	505,000	127	197	135	1927
12 3	12 10½	1,099,000 j	374,000	80	261,000	63	206	147	1928
12 0	12 5¼	1,314,000 k	477,000	100	423,000	100	201	152	1929
10 10	11 6¾	1,264,000	636,000	130	1,419,000	328	189	157	1930
10 10	11 7¾	1,288,000	926,000	182	854,000	190	162	147	1931
10 10	11 2½	1,331,000	769,000	145	1,359,000	289	125	132	1932
10 10	10 10	1,357,000 j	379,000	69	265,000	54	123	147	1933
10 10	10 10	1,427,000	318,000	58	293,000	61	118	147	1934
10 6	10 10¼	1,466,000	424,000	78	881,000	189	126	152	1935
10 3	11 2¾	1,501,000	756,000	144	575,000	131	108	156	1936
10 8	11 7	1,538,000	873,000	176	681,000	166	105	167	1937
10 8	11 7	1,580,000 j	779,000	157	408,000	100	92	164	1938
11 0	12 2	1,632,000	650,000	..	440,000	..	..	..	1939

g Figures for 1920 and 1921 are for domiciliary relief other than on account of sickness, accident and bodily or mental infirmity.

h Bar indicates annexation of parishes from South Stoneham Union.

i Bars indicate transfer of responsibility, in two stages, for the able-bodied unemployed to the Unemployment Assistance Board.

j Bars indicate rating reassessments.

k Bar indicates total derating of agricultural land and partial derating of industrial properties.

l Includes £426,000 for the purchase of undertakings from Hampshire Water Authority.

SOURCES

A *The Registrar General's Statistical Review of England and Wales*, Tables, pt II, Civil, 1919-39.

B Ministry of Labour, *Local Employment Index*, 1927-39; Minutes of evidence (days 10 and 11) of the Ministry of Labour to *The Royal Commission on the Geographical Distribution of the Industrial Population*, Non-Parliamentary Papers, 1938, appendix I, table xxxii, p. 314; National Health Insurance statistics for 1919 and 1921 from the *Southampton Times*.

C Calculated from weekly returns printed in the local press for 1921 and 1922 and from monthly returns in *The Ministry of Labour Gazette*, 1923-39.

D Recalculated from sources as for B and C.

E *British labour statistics, historical abstract, 1886-1968* (HMSO, 1971) table 160, p. 306.

F, G, H, I Annual *Statement of the number of persons in receipt of poor law relief on the night of 1st January, BPP*, 1919-39.

J, K County Borough of Southampton, *Abstract of the Treasurer's Accounts* for the years ending 1919-39.

L *Annual local taxation returns, England and Wales, pt II*, Non-Parliamentary Papers, Ministry of Health, 1920-39.

M, N As J.

O Based on index of prices in Alan T Peacock and Jack Wiseman, *The growth of public expenditure in the United Kingdom* (Oxford UP, 1961) table A-3, pp. 155-6.

P As J.

Q As O.

R *The Ministry of Labour Gazette*, 1921-39.

S *Annual Statement of the Navigation and Shipping of the United Kingdom, BPP*, 1921, XXXIV, Cd 1419 and 1442; Non-Parliamentary Papers, Board of Trade, 1922-39.

APPENDIX 3

COMPOSITION OF SOUTHAMPTON COUNTY BOROUGH COUNCIL, 1919-38

	Independent	Labour
1919	(40)[a]	12
1920[b]	56	12
1921	55	13
1922	60	8
1923	58	10
1924	60	8
1925	57	11
1926	57	11
1927	56	12
1928	53	15
1929	48	19
1930	48	20
1931	52	16
1932	51	17
1933	47	21
1934	43	25
1935	43	25
1936	43	25
1937	43	25
1938	43	25

SOURCE *Hampshire Advertiser*, 1919-39.

NOTES a 30 Conservatives, 3 Liberals and 7 independents.

b Additional membership consequent on the extension of the borough.

THE VOLUNTARY RESPONSE TO MASS UNEMPLOYMENT IN SOUTH WALES

Peter Stead

There has been no political revolution in twentieth-century Britain and it is therefore very tempting to see the triumph of political consensus as the major theme of this period. The general absence of open conflict and political discontinuity, however, has rather disguised quite considerable differences between various groups at particular points in time and the social historian of contemporary Britain ought not to ignore these moments when groups with differing beliefs, values and perspectives have come into direct confrontation. British society in this century has continued to consist of quite distinct sub-cultures and, in spite of an absence of revolution and of open violence, contact and conflict between sub-cultures has often revealed political and social differences quite as marked as those in countries with more violent political traditions.

The General Strike of 1926 afforded perhaps the most spectacular example of differing social perspectives within British society. The outcome of the Strike was undoubtedly a triumph for political consensus but, at the time, few people were left unaware of the mammoth differences in ideology, perspective and life-style between various groups in society. Lord Birkenhead's famous judgement on the miners' leaders, that 'I should call them the stupidest men in England if I had not previously had to deal with the owners', nicely indicated how far apart were the three main groups in the national negotiations but it was social differences which were revealed quite as much as political or industrial differences.[1] The Strike conditioned responses from groups who seemed to have come from different planets rather than from different parts of the same country as the miners. W H Auden, a student at Oxford during the Strike, was later to admit that, at the time, 'it had never occurred to me that anybody took the General Strike seriously'. His explanation of the alacrity with which many students rushed to help the Government was that 'neither Marx nor any other social anatomist had spotted that it was the day-dream of almost every middle-class English boy to drive a train or bus, to do something which his social position normally forbade, like loading a ship or directing traffic'. Auden saw this sort of response as the fulfillment of a dream rather than a display of 'class consciousness in the Marxist sense' but was also forced to admit that it was a response rooted in political ignorance and indifference.[2]

This ignorance and indifference were to disappear in the aftermath of the General Strike and one can argue that British working-class and trade union politics were never to be quite as remote from intellectual and middle-class life as they had been in the mid-1920s.

1 Quoted in Alan J P Taylor, *English history 1914-1945* (Oxford: Clarendon Press, 1965) p. 141.

2 Wystan H Auden, 'As it seemed to us', *The New Yorker*, 3 April 1965, reprinted in *Forewords and afterwards* (Faber, 1973) pp. 492-524.

Slowly but surely after 1926 the working-class presence was absorbed into the cultural debate and by the mid-1930s a new chapter in the story of intellectual responses to the working-class had begun.[1] There was no longer an excuse for ignorance and the whole dynamic of the culture was against indifference. The facts of social division and of widely differing social experiences were now widely appreciated and openly discussed and every effort was made to mould a politics and a culture that could absorb and allow for information and such analysis. A new populism developed as newsreels, documentary films, new journals and magazines and a whole new literature highlighted and yet sought to hold together the varying social groups that made up British society.

The period of the Great Depression was characterised, therefore, by a process in which social awareness and social analysis began to play a more important role within the culture. The ignorance and indifference of 1926 had been decisively abandoned but this did not necessarily mean that the varying sub-cultures came closer to understanding and appreciating each other's beliefs and values. The erosion of ignorance and indifference still left room for considerable misunderstanding. The new interest in the working-class, which did so much to characterise the 1930s as a decade, was more often than not a product of forces determined within the logic of other social groups rather than evidence that those groups and the working-class had moved closer together. This was most clearly revealed in the new relationship which developed between artists, writers and intellectuals generally and the working-class. In the Documentary movement, whether in film or literature, the subject of the worker and his life-style became a touchstone for the artist to work out new values and new techniques.[2] Similarly, for left-wing intellectuals, the fact of working-class wholesomeness and integrity allowed them to construct a new set of political values in the face of new and complex international forces.[3] The middle-class were behaving very differently from the way they had behaved in 1926 but this new emphasis on social empathy and on solidarity with the proletariat was almost as much an indication of social differences as were the responses of 1926. There was merely a new pattern of relationships between sub-cultures.

In the years before the international dangers of Fascism were fully appreciated it was the fact of mass unemployment which did most to condition new responses to the working-class. Society had to come to terms with the enormity of the problem and then, in turn, with its many implications. The statistics were all too familiar and it could be argued that no previous social problem had ever been so painstakingly enumerated. Behind the national figure of almost 3 million unemployed at the bottom of the Depression were the implications of the even more frightening local statistics. It became widely known that there were

1 Adrian Mellor, Chris Pawling and Colin Sparks, 'Writers and the General Strike' in Margaret Morris, *The General Strike* (Harmondsworth: Penguin, 1976) pp. 338-57.

2 William Stott, *Documentary expression and thirties America* (New York: Oxford UP, 1973).

3 Samuel Hynes, *The Auden generation: literature and politics in England in the 1930s* (Bodley Head, 1976).

communities, such as Jarrow and Merthyr, where over 60 per cent of the workforce were unemployed and then, as time went on, it became appreciated that there were many men who had not worked for years. In the Rhondda of 1936 there were 11,000 men who had been continuously out of work for over a year. In South Wales as a whole the figures for 1934 revealed that 52 per cent of the wholly unemployed had been unemployed for over two years and 10.8 per cent had been unemployed for more than five years.[1] Statistics such as these were repeated in report after report and became the basis not so much of a political but more of a cultural response. Employment and the wages that it produced had been so basic to the industrial economy that society soon realised that it was confronted with a totally new problem. Clearly the implications of life without work and within a new set of economic sanctions had to be analysed and faced-up-to as soon as possible. So revolutionary and so singular was this new social experience that the national culture had necessarily to create a debate on its ramifications. It was necessary for mass and long-term unemployment to be understood within the accepted norms and values of the culture. In this sense, the cultural problem of unemployment played a very similar role to that played by the problem of poverty in late-Victorian England. In both cases the straight-forward horror resulting from an objective appreciation of deprivation and hardship was only one element in a more complex culture-shock which had its origin in the realisation that lives were being lived outside what were thought to be the norms of social existence. In both cases, the energy that was subsequently channelled into estimating the extent of deprivation, into analysing its implications and into organising remedial action was only in part motivated by an altruistic concern and sympathy, for culture-shocks tend to generate their own energy and tend to direct people into efforts aimed at resolving apparent paradoxes within their society. Victorian evangelicism mutated into a fascination with poverty without very greatly changing the predominant values and certainly without doing much that interfered with the root-causes of that poverty. Similarly in the 1930s the unemployed occasioned a whole range of responses which allow us to take stock of the culture but which did not, on the whole, enable the unemployed themselves to enter a new Jerusalem.[2]

What happened in the 1930s was that a feeling developed that something urgently needed to be done for the unemployed as individuals and, even more perhaps, for the communities in which the unemployed were concentrated. This response was experienced first by activists in voluntary movements and, following their pioneer efforts, an official and general view developed that efforts on behalf of the unemployed were needed and were, in fact, best handled by independent and voluntary organisations. It may well be that, as the Russell Committee on Adult Education of 1973 argued, 'in any free society voluntaryism is inherent' for certainly voluntary movements concerned with social amelioration and the provision of social services were well-established

1 Ministry of Labour, *Reports of Investigations into the industrial conditions in certain depressed areas*, III. *South Wales and Monmouthshire*, 1934.

2 For role of poverty see Gareth Steadman Jones, *Outcast London: a study in the relationship between classes in Victorian society* (Oxford: Clarendon Press, 1971).

in Victorian and Edwardian Britain.[1] The conscious restraints placed on governmental action, the need to give concrete expression to notions of class interdependence and the need to channel the energies of reformers had firmly established voluntaryism as the method best suited to coping with social problems and resolving contradictions within society. Historians, of course, have gradually been showing how charity, philanthropy and the closely-associated method of voluntaryism have played significant social roles in almost every historical era but it may still come as a surprise that the twentieth-century experience of mass-unemployment should give rise to another flowering of the voluntary tradition. Indeed the inter-war years in Britain were to provide one of the most significant, as well as perhaps the last, chapter in the history of voluntaryism in Britain. One historian of voluntary social action has spoken of a 'new spate of generosity' after 1928. The opening of the new chapter can perhaps be dated more precisely. It was in June 1926 that the Quaker Emma Noble first went to the Rhondda and realised that old industrial areas of the country were in dire need of a new kind of social service. Her vision and enthusiasm were conveyed to the Friends at Oxford and they resolved to help the Rhondda by providing relief and by organising self-help efforts. In 1927 Emma Noble and her husband William were able to supervise the opening of a permanent centre for this work at Maes-yr-Haf, Trealaw in mid-Rhondda. Known as the Maes-yr-Haf Educational Settlement, it represented the beginning of a whole new response to industrial poverty and in particular to mass unemployment.[2]

What Maes-yr-Haf established was a pattern of dealing with the unemployed whereby voluntary organisations offered a package in which relief took the form of practical aids such as the provision of seeds and of tools, in which an emphasis was placed on training people for new crafts and then on using those crafts in enterprises run on a co-operative basis where the whole families of the unemployed were taught to fend for themselves, in which people were taught to think of ways in which work-schemes would benefit their local community and in which practical work was combined with a range of adult education classes. At Maes-yr-Haf, too, the pattern was set of young and talented men and women, mainly from the universities and in particular from Balliol College, Oxford, giving their time to work with unemployed miners in towns and villages which they would never previously have visited. This formula, which emerged in the Rhondda in the 1920s, set the pattern for most of what was to follow on a national scale during the 1930s.

At very much the same time another experiment was taking place at Brynmawr, on the northern boundary of industrial South Wales. Here the concept was if anything even bolder, although not as influential as Maes-yr-Haf. The two experiments together illustrated that something should and could be done for these blighted communities. At Brynmawr Peter Scott and other Quakers had followed an initial visit in 1928 by the founding in 1929 of a centre for relief work. What was to

1 *Committee of Inquiry into Adult Education: a plan for development* (Department of Education and Science Committee of Inquiry (Russell Report) HMSO, 1973) p. 76.

2 Kathleen Butterworth, *William Noble and his wife Emma* (Friends Home Service Committee, 1962).

distinguish the work at Brynmawr was the way in which the Quakers invited members of the local community to join with them in organising co-operative work-schemes to provide employment and to form the basis for a regeneration of the whole community. The outcome was a spate of co-operative schemes and the formation in 1932 of An Order of Friends to provide leadership and direction in this bold attempt to create an alternative society in one isolated industrial village. Few other communities ever went this far but throughout the 1930s Brynmawr was widely regarded as the cutting-edge of social experiment and of voluntary relief work.[1]

The new chapter in the history of voluntary work started with these two small groups of Quakers in the years immediately prior to what is normally thought of as the Great Depression proper. It was only in 1929 that the deprivation and distress that had been diagnosed in Welsh industrial communities became a more general phenomenon and one demanding a national response. Now bodies other than the Society of Friends began to see the urgent need of channelling monies into the areas badly hit by unemployment. The story of those years was one of increased expenditure by existing bodies and of a rallying around to support the more worthwhile experiments being carried out at the local level. There really was a remarkable quickening of pace in 1929. That year saw the coming together of the two most important institutions in the sphere of voluntary social effort. The Carnegie United Kingdom Trust, which had been financing new amenities for working-class areas since 1913, was approached by the National Council of Social Service, which had been founded during the period of reconstruction after the war, to help finance new educational experiments amongst the unemployed in South Wales and the north-east. From this small beginning both organisations were launched into major new roles which kept them at the centre of the national response throughout the 1930s with the Carnegie Trust, in particular, continuously on the look-out for new experiments to support. Then in 1930 a letter in *The Times* announced that a Mr Edward Harkness of New York had placed in the hands of trustees 'a large sum of money, which he desires should be spent for the benefit of Great Britain'. So there came into being the Pilgrim Trust, which although equally concerned with the restoration and upkeep of Britain's architectural heritage, became famous in the 1930s for the way in which it supported schemes to help the unemployed. Its first report recorded how 'the Trustees felt that they must respond to the repeated appeals which were reaching them to assist agencies which were working to counteract some of the worse effects of continued unemployment' and, with this end in view, they too contacted the NCSS to see whether some national scheme could be organised.[2] Both the Carnegie and Pilgrim Trusts were looking to the NCSS, which they thought of as the best national co-ordinating body, and they expressed a desire to work with the NCSS to choose the most worthwhile local efforts.

Meanwhile local efforts were mushrooming as other centres, settlements, training schemes, holiday camps, allotment schemes, education classes, hostels and youth clubs were coming into existence

1 Society of Friends, *An Order of Friends: an account of their activities and ideas* (Hereford, 1936).

2 The Pilgrim Trust, *First Annual Report 1930-1931*.

under the auspices of local committees, local councils of social service, the YMCA, the Boys Brigade and so on. All over the country now the unemployed were being encouraged to come together to learn new skills, to launch co-operative efforts, to work in the construction of new amenities such as playing fields and swimming pools, to participate in cultural activities such as choirs and amateur dramatics, to send their young to clubs and camps and their wives to domestic science classes. To organise and supervise these activities there emerged two new and distinct groups. At the local level one found what we may term the social workers: the graduates, the Quakers, the idealists giving their time to instruct and to organise. At the national level one found an expanding but still quite small group of people who administered the NCSS and the various trusts, who sat on executives and on co-ordinating committees and who, with their combination of experience, administrative know-how and social and political connections, were emerging as an influential national lobby. They stood at the head of this voluntary movement; it was they who determined which were the worthwhile experiments and it was they, who by publicly defining the meaning, value and role of voluntary social service, gave shape to a new force within national life. It was Emma Noble, Peter Scott and their colleagues who pioneered the new approach to unemployment but, by the early 1930s, it was men like Thomas Jones of the Pilgrim Trust, Colonel Mitchell of the Carnegie Trust and Captain Ellis of the NCSS who were giving voluntary effort its overall form and its national identity.[1]

The basic formula that emerged between 1929 and 1932 was to continue for the rest of the decade, although, of course there was increased expenditure and there were changes of emphasis in the light of increased information revealed in the investigations into the nature of unemployment which many of the trusts commissioned.[2] The one major change in the formula came in November 1932 when the government decided to ask the NCSS to act as the central advisory body with regard to voluntary schemes and, in addition, made a grant of £10,000 to the NCSS to be used in assisting such schemes amongst the unemployed. In December the Prime Minister, Ramsay MacDonald, gave a broadcast talk to justify this new departure in government policy. He referred to the way in which 'for years now public-spirited men have been labouring with, and on behalf of, the unemployed in those areas where the heavy hand of industrial depression is still'. The government were convinced that there was 'still a source of wealth in personal service' and so itself was now seeking to help and encourage 'further co-operation and activity in voluntary service for the unemployed'. He saw this initiative as 'an attempt on a national scale to find new ways of employment, to put a new spirit of co-operation and independence into our people, so that through distress and failure we may find a way to national unity and commonwealth well-being'.[3] Many supporters of the

1 The sense of this new movement is best conveyed in the respective annual reports and in William Robertson, *Welfare in trust: a history of the Carnegie United Kingdom Trust 1913-1963* (Dunfermline: Carnegie United Kingdom Trust, 1964).

2 See John Stevenson, *Social conditions in Britain between the wars* (Harmondsworth: Penguin, 1977) for extracts from the most important investigations.

3 *The Times*, 20 December 1932.

NCSS were distressed by this windfall which they thought would necessarily weaken the voluntary spirit and there were others who argued that the NCSS by tradition had a much broader role to play than the mere relief of the unemployed. The majority of supporters however saw this as an exciting moment in the history of the National Council and were determined to use this opportunity to launch an even greater national effort. In this new dispensation an increasingly important role was played by the Prince of Wales, the Patron of the NCSS, who by the mid-1930s had in many ways become the national symbol of this new effort which was combining public and private monies and bringing together statutory and voluntary social service. The status of the National Council was transformed. In 1927 its total expenditure had been £4430, of which some £2500 had been donated by the Carnegie Trust. In 1933 the Charities Account of the NCSS distributed some £218,000 and during the two years 1933-5 its income from the Ministry of Labour alone totalled almost £80,000.[1]

A few people had launched a new approach to the problem of unemployment and had then seen this transformed into a national and official response, a response which, under the patronage of the Prince of Wales, was to receive a tremendous amount of publicity in both press and newsreels throughout the 1930s. 'A characteristic of the times was its active social conscience' was the summing up of C L Mowat and this response to unemployment forms a significant clue to the whole nature of British society during those years. It was a response which, of course, depended on the unemployed themselves being willing to co-operate and willing to receive help and instruction. This co-operation was forthcoming and the unemployed in significant numbers learned to mend boots, to cultivate allotments, to construct swimming pools, to analyse novels, to sing in choirs, to make their own clothes and to run co-operative enterprises. It was, in particular, the unemployed clubs which tended to develop out of centres and settlements which brought the rank-and-file unemployed under the influence of the social workers. In 1936 there were 183,000 unemployed persons in South Wales at a time when there were 257 unemployed clubs with a membership in the region of 27,000.[2] As of course the NCSS maintained, 'the real story of what is happening . . . is not told in a recital of statistics', for what was more important was that in nearly every community which had been destroyed by unemployment there had been established an organisation which was encouraging a whole new range of activities. There was a new dynamic, a new source of energy. Those active in the NCSS and the Settlements were fired by a tremendous enthusiasm for the success of these clubs and were excited, not only by the diversion and relief that they were now offering the unemployed but also by a feeling that they had stumbled on to a new type of social organisation and to a new focus of social activity within industrial areas. By 1939 the NCSS saw such clubs as pioneering the way to a system of 'permanent social-service clubs'.[3]

1 Margaret Brasnett, *Voluntary social action: a history of the National Council of Social Service, 1919-1969* (NCSS, 1969) pp. 55, 78.

2 *Voluntary service in South Wales: Second Annual Report of the South Wales and Monmouthshire Council of Social Service, 1935-1936.*

3 National Council of Social Service, *Out of adversity: a survey of the clubs for men and women which have grown out of the needs of unemployment* (London, 1939).

Throughout the decade the voluntary movement was proud of what it had achieved and was openly congratulating itself on the worthiness of its response. Nevertheless this always tended to be accompanied by a qualifying defensiveness with regard to the movement's record of success, for the advocates and supporters of voluntary response knew that their efforts had been sustained in the face of much suspicion and not a little open hostility. Things had happened dramatically and there was always some unease about the way in which the government had stepped in, about the way in which institutions had moved away from their original intentions and about the way in which they had been forced to co-operate with erstwhile rivals. There was always what Margaret Brasnett summed up as a 'tension of ideas within the movement' but, whatever the relationship between the agencies themselves, the main source of this tension was the relationship between the voluntary movement on the one hand and the community of the unemployed on the other. The unemployed themselves had many reservations about the voluntary efforts made on their behalf and these reservations were reinforced and articulated by a number of organisations. These included the National Unemployed Workers Movement, which claimed to be the national voice of the unemployed, the political parties such as the Labour Party, the ILP and the Communist Party, the vast bulk of the trade union movement and many Labour-controlled local authorities who tended to be extremely jealous of these new organisations which had sprouted-up within the areas of their own jurisdiction. The voluntary movement had powerful enemies who ensured sustained public criticism and a lack of co-operation. The movement had forged an alliance of social workers, the government and private benefactors but it was never able to recruit support from the organised left, from the trade union movement and from many of the key local authorities.

The paradox was that the voluntary movement was convinced that it was relieving distress and organising worthwhile activities, whilst many of the unemployed and many organisations, who regarded the unemployed as forming their natural constituencies, felt apathetic or hostile towards the whole phenomenon. This difference in outlook and judgement was a highly complex matter and one which, in bringing together political, regional and class values, allows us to capture nicely many of the elements making up the national culture. Thoughout, of course, the sharpest note of criticism and the most uncompromising hostility was motivated by political considerations. The straightforward and very convincing argument of the Left was that unemployment was a political or economic question and, therefore, would only be solved by those in authority choosing the right options and devising the right policies. Relief work and charitable enterprise could only cloud the issue and syphon-off energy from the all important political demand - that the government should provide jobs for all. Year in and year out the Left repeated its view that mass unemployment had resulted from an 'unsound economic position, created by the present system of production and distribution'. This was a crisis in the history of capitalism and, quite apart from the need for new and generous measures of unemployment assistance, the fundamental imperative was 'the complete abolition of the system of production for profit and the substitution of a system based upon Socialist Economy'.[1] The

1 The Socialist 'classic' of the 1930s is Allen Hutt, *The condition of the working class in Britain* (Martin Lawrence, 1933). In his introduction, Harry Pollitt said that 'on the basis of a Socialist planned economy every idle pit, factory and shipyard in the country could be set going'.

crisis demanded political action and this action had to be taken by the workers and the unemployed themselves. The capture of political power was the urgent need of the hour. This viewpoint was advocated most strongly by the Communist Party and the National Unemployed Workers' Movement which was closely connected with the Communist Party. These were never anything but small movements; it has been estimated that in 1932 only 3140 out of a total of 2.7 million unemployed were members of the Communist Party and that NUWM never mobilised more than 10 per cent of the unemployed at any one time.[1] In a sense, though, these are misleading figures, for there is a way in which both the Communist Party and the NUWM did emerge as authentic voices of the unemployed both within certain communities and at a national level. Wal Hannington, the leader and publicist of the NUWM, who as early as 1923 was referred to by *The Guardian* as 'The Napoleon of the unemployed', succeeded in creating a feeling in the 1930s that there was a self-generated working-class movement protesting against unemployment. A Cabinet memorandum of 1936 warned that there was a danger of the Communists creating the impression that Hunger Marches represented a 'mass struggle of the unemployed' and this fear points to the way in which small organisations did have an influence and indeed a legitimacy which was greater than their numbers suggested.[2]

In the 1930s the Communists, though few in number, articulated the views of many. Many of the unemployed undoubtedly understood and agreed with the scathing attack made on the NCSS in 1933 by the Communist writer Allen Hutt who spoke of the social services as 'doping the unemployed' and of 'bread and circuses' as being the 'classical formula for successfully continuing the oppression of the plebs in order to maintain the politicians in power'.[3] What gave credence to the Communist argument was that the NCSS and its associates rose to prominence at precisely the moment when the government launched a new chapter in the story of unemployment relief, a chapter above all symbolised by the means test and summed up by Hannington in the following terms: 'Capitalism, which has taken huge profits and wealth from the sweat and toil of these people in the basic industries of the country, is now crucifying them'.[4] There were many unemployed and many in the Labour movement who felt that 'the Means Test . . . has been the cause of more misery and unhappiness than any other piece of legislation in modern times' and appreciated the incongruity of government grants to the NCSS at a time when £15 million was taken back from the unemployed.[5] It may well have been only a few workers and intellectuals who fully saw the relevance

1 Kenneth Newton, *The sociology of British Communism* (Allen Lane, 1969) p. 34.

2 *The Guardian*, 5 February 1923. This story on Hannington is in the Home Office Files (HO 45/11275). For Cabinet Memorandum of 12 October 1936, see Cabinet 57, 256.

3 Hutt, *Condition*, p. 185.

4 Walter Hannington, *The problem of the distressed areas* (Gollancz, 1937) p. 76.

5 Griff Roberts, *Unemployment: reflections of a victim* (Llwchwr Labour Party, 1936).

of Hannington's claim that 'in the midst of a capitalist world where 50 million persons are unemployed stands the one great country, Soviet Russia, where under the rule of the workers, unemployment has been solved'[1] but many more would have shared his inability to believe 'that those, who keep the unemployed on a scale of benefit which means starvation, and then snatch every penny they can from them under the means test, are the friends of the unemployed when they offer them recreation instead of bread'.[2]

For the most part those active in voluntary movements were not noted for their involvement in the political movements which claimed to represent the unemployed and the working-class. Certainly the Society of Friends consistently spoke out against social evils and urged their members to seek means of moving towards 'a New Social Order'. In 1931 Peter Scott argued that the 10 per cent reduction in unemployment benefit had 'shown that this margin, small though it may seem to be, makes all the difference between the subsistence level and acute poverty'[3] and in 1936 a Friends' pamphlet roundly denounced the operation of the means test as 'disastrous'.[4] Friends, though, operated within the logic and ethic of their own movement and did not in any way create a link between the voluntary movement and the socialist parties. Far more important now, in any case, were the national leaders of voluntary effort and there would have been many who would have appreciated Hannington's listing of the leaders of the NCSS in 1932 and then his subsequent assertion that 'I think we should search in vain for any evidence of these honoured gentlemen ever having associated themselves with the demand for the abolition of the means test and the restoration of benefit cuts'.

Voluntary effort went on in a context of continual sniping from the Left. This opposition was always expressed most forcibly by Communists but was frequently shared by many in the Labour Party, who could with more justification claim to speak on behalf of unemployed communities. In Parliament itself it was individual Labour members who continually expressed the viewpoint of the unemployed and in so doing made clear their suspicion of the new prominence being given to voluntary effort. They were confronted by members of the government who took pains to praise the social work that was being done and to stress the significance. Sir Henry Betterton, the Minister of Labour responsible for the first grant to the NCSS, spoke of all those who were 'sincerely anxious to help' the unemployed and promised on several occasions that, in encouraging voluntary work, the government were not 'attempting to avoid our responsibility in other directions'.[5] The immediate response of many on the opposition benches were summed up by George Buchanan, ILP member for the Gorbals. He viewed 'this grant

1 Walter Hannington, *Unemployed to action* (National Union of Unemployed Workers, nd) p. 14.

2 Hannington, *Distressed areas*, p. 198.

3 Royal Commission on Unemployment Insurance 1931, Memorandum by Mr Peter Scott, 31 December 1931.

4 *The Means Test* (Society of Friends' Industrial and Social Order Council, 1936).

5 *Parliamentary Debates (Hansard)*, 19 December 1932.

with a great deal of suspicion and a good deal of hostility'. In the following months most Labour members who spoke on the subject of voluntary effort emphasised how inappropriate for dealing with unemployment was anything that smacked of charity. Ramsay MacDonald had begged his listeners to 'separate all those things . . . from the idea of giving something in charity' but this was precisely the note taken up in the House. George Lansbury admitted that helping people was one matter but that he was ashamed 'when every night I have to face a poster, going home on the Underground Railway, appealing for any unemployed clothes to go to the unemployed men'. He argued that it was 'a disgrace for the British Government to throw this on the shoulders of private charity'. The most outspoken MPs were from South Wales; George Dagger summed up the NCSS grants (which amounted to £15,000 in 1933, or 1½d per unemployed man at a time when benefit was being cut by 1s 8d a week) as 'studied insults to the unemployed' and Nye Bevan brilliantly countered accusations of ingratitude by reminding Lady Astor and those who shared her view that Socialism could not do better that 'I have never contended that the difference between a Conservative and myself is that I love my neighbour any the more strongly than he does. All I have said about the Conservatives is not that he is less humanitarian, but simply that he is more stupid'.[1]

Accusations of charity were perhaps even more telling than the more controversial socialist critique forwarded by the Communists. Working-men who had all their lives prided themselves on their financial independence were hardly likely to be enthusiastic about accepting relief and being recruited into a new kind of labour but, over and above their own sense of independence, they would not have been impressed by many aspects of the publicity surrounding voluntary schemes. Many were disconcerted by what was quite consistently advanced as the main motive of our relief work. However much sympathy there was with the fact of hardship and poverty, there was always a tremendous emphasis in voluntary literature on what we may best categorise as the 'moral problems' consequent upon unemployment. The Pilgrim Trust in their survey *Men without work* summed these up as 'questions concerning the effects of unemployment on men's sense of self-respect and their attitude towards society in general, questions which are partly psychological in character, partly moral'.[2] Nearly all outside observers who recorded reactions to unemployment were to emphasise that the greatest tragedy of unemployment was its impact on social relationships. E Wight Bakke diagnosed a collapse of 'the normal structure of societal living' and a reduction of 'the reality of citizenship'.[3] Bakke pointed to the growing isolation of each unemployed person as they lost 'contact with organisations which participate to some extent in the larger interests of the community'

1 *Parliamentary Debates*, Mr George Buchanan, 19 December 1932; Mr George Lansbury and Mr George Dagger, 16 February 1933, Mr Aneurin Bevan, 27 April 1933.

2 *Men without work: a report made to the Pilgrim Trust* (Cambridge UP, 1938) p. 180.

3 Edward Wight Bakke, *Citizens without work: a study of the effects of unemployment upon the workers' social relations and practices* (New Haven, Conn: Yale UP, 1940) pp. 16, 305.

and maintained that an attitude of 'put up with it, grin and bear it' kept the unemployed away from 'political group action'. The Pilgrim Trust's first report spoke of how 'in the valleys of the South Wales coalfield there are thousands of boys living in idleness, not knowing how to get through the long day and falling into mischief from boredom. Good material is running to waste for lack of the interest and discipline which come from useful occupation'. Its second report pointed to 'the deterioration, physical and technical, of the worker condemned to long periods of idleness'.[1] In her famous study of Brynmawr, Hilda Jennings stated very succinctly what was the view of most social workers in the 1930s; for her 'the tragedy of unemployment in the distressed areas chiefly consists not in material want but in the loss of belief in these non-material values which differentiate man from the animal'.[2]

Throughout the 1930s there was much talk of 'character' and 'independence' and the unemployed were made all too aware that there were those who were more concerned with their moral worth than with how much money they had in their pockets. A *Times* editorial of 1930 had talked of how 'the transcendent importance of character should be more generally discerned in our public life' and of how the one road back to prosperity was 'to regain self-discipline and self-reliance, an honest pride in work and clean patriotism'.[3] Such attitudes seemed all too closely related to the question of whether the unemployed were genuinely seeking work and to the Pilgrim Trust's assertion that the fact that there were 'a certain number of "work-shy" men among the younger unemployed is, of course, not open to doubt'.[4] There was every reason to believe that the total lack of employment prospects had a disastrous impact on young people for this emerged as the best documented aspect of the Depression[5] but the continued emphasis on 'decline' and 'idleness' did little to win the unemployed over to the side of the voluntary workers.

What was often thought was best expressed in the House of Commons by George Buchanan. He agreed that there was physical deterioration but he had failed to detect that 'moral deterioration of the unemployed' of which there was so much talk. He told the House that he knew 'men who are married and have two children and who have never worked in their lives, and they are good men, good husbands, clean intelligent citizens. Then we find supercilious people, who have always had assured incomes, talking about deterioration'. His argument was that the unemployed would 'utilise their time better than any other person can utilise it for them'. The unemployed would form their own associations and devise their own institutions and pressure-groups; they did not need patronage but 'income, and given income, they will make life decent and happy

1 The Pilgrim Trust, *Second Annual Report*, 1932.

2 Hilda Jennings, *Brynmawr: a study of a distressed area* (Brynmawr Community Study Council, 1934) p. 142.

3 *The Times*, 1 January 1930.

4 *Men without work*, p. 173.

5 See, for example, Archibald J Lush, *The young adult: being a report prepared in co-operation with young men in Cardiff, Newport and Pontypridd, under the auspices of the Carnegie United Kingdom Trust* (Cardiff: South Wales and Monmouthshire Council of Social Service, 1941) and *Disinherited youth: a report on the 18+ age group enquiry* (Edinburgh: Constable, 1943); Edward S Conway, *Post-war employment* (Cape, 1943).

for themselves'.[1] Wal Hannington went even further than this and argued that voluntary effort motivated by this fear of deterioration could, if anything, lead to 'demoralisation' amongst the unemployed. He defined demoralisation as being a state in which one was 'deprived of courage and self-reliance' and he saw this 'as precisely the state of mind which is produced by the charity approach to the question of unemployment by the social service centres'.[2]

This emphasis on moral questions and this concern with the morale of the unemployed often seemed related to two other notions which in turn caused misgivings on the left and amongst the unemployed. We saw earlier that the Pilgrim Trust talked of the 'discipline' which came from useful occupation. Such observations did much to encourage people to associate voluntary schemes with what was seen as a growing use of compulsion in government policy. Nothing did more in the 1930s to turn the unemployed against government relief measures than the way in which official reports increasingly stressed the need for compulsion and the way in which more and more strings were being attached to relief and training, especially of young people. In 1938 the Commissioner for the Special Areas looked at the question of payments to those over sixteen and concluded that it seemed 'reasonable to attach to the receipt of these payments such conditions as are calculated to create or preserve physical fitness and to improve the morale of that small class of young applicants who are so lacking in initiative that they will not take advantage of the opportunities which are open to them'.[3] This kind of language horrified the unemployed. Wal Hannington's *The problem of the distressed areas*, published in 1937, is well-known as the most strongly-worded attack on government compulsion and on the institutionalisation of training. He talked of 'slave camps' and of the unemployed being treated as if they were 'a lower species of humanity'. He described in detail 'the semi-military discipline' at the camps. For all his extremism, Hannington was giving voice to the fears of many. There was amongst the unemployed a deep-seated resistance to having to submit to residence away from home and few could ever understand the importance consistently attached to physical training which invariably came under the supervision of ex-military types.

What concerns us here is that some people undoubtedly associated voluntary training schemes with the drift towards compulsion in official policy. In his study Hannington did his best to establish this connection. He showed that the 1934 act, which introduced the regulations allowing attendance at centres to be made compulsory for those unemployed coming under the UAB, was introduced precisely at a time when pressure was being placed on voluntary agencies to provide occupational training and physical training centres.[4] There were undoubtedly social workers in the 1930s who wanted to see greater powers of compulsion. In 1943 Edward Conway was to write of the young people that 'they should be compelled to use their time profitably'.[5]

1 *Parliamentary Debates*, 19 December 1932.

2 Hannington, *Distressed areas*, p. 212.

3 Commissioner for the Special Areas Report 1938, p. 9.

4 Hannington, *Distressed areas*, p. 197 et seq.

5 Conway, *Post-war employment*, p. 93.

Hannington's attempt to associate voluntary centres with compulsion may well have convinced some but in a way the very fact that these centres were run by voluntary organisations saved them at the local level. There was probably much frustration amongst social workers as they encountered the informality and irregularity of the unemployed but many probably saw the advantage that accrued, as Miss Jennings put it, from avoiding 'any suggestion of external force' and of developing the potential 'to appeal for the free co-operation of the persons whose social capacity it is desired to promote'.[1]

The second notion with which a concern with 'deterioration' could be related was that of an interest in leadership amongst the unemployed. The first report of the Pilgrim Trust hoped that its programme of relief would 'prevent many places where moral and intellectual leadership is absent from sinking into despair'.[2] This lack of leadership amongst the unemployed was to be a particular concern of the Pilgrim Trust reflecting the specific interests of its secretary, Thomas Jones. Jones, who had been a Deputy Secretary to the Cabinet before joining the Pilgrim Trust, was one of a small but influential group who advanced the claims of adult education in the 1920s and 1930s and who succeeded in making adult education one of the main preoccupations of all those concerned in voluntary work with the unemployed.[3] Through their efforts, adult education classes became available at the local level on an unprecedented scale and, at the national level, bodies such as the Education Settlements Association, the WEA, the NCSS, the educational trusts and the residential colleges (such as the college at Harlech which Jones had founded in 1927) were creating what was, in effect, a new national system of adult education. There was, of course, massive educational deprivation and few doubted the need for and value of adult education but throughout the period there was resentment in some quarters that adult classes were being provided by voluntary movements and that this education was so closely associated with the other so-called 'charitable activities' sponsored by those movements. Consequently, this splendid adult education network which developed was often forced to recruit its students from a rather narrower range than it would have liked but, without doubt, its own emphasis on the need for leaders contributed to this. Most potential students were interested in education for its own sake rather than for developing powers of leadership and certainly they never saw themselves as a potential source of an alternative leadership to the existing leaders in the labour and trade-union movement. The voluntary adult education movement contributed much that was worthwhile but never rid itself of restricting ambiguities in its outlook. Such ambiguities necessarily created misunderstanding. In 1934 the Secretary of the Rhos Unemployed Welfare Association in North Wales wrote to the Warden of Coleg Harlech with the news that 'no person from amongst the unemployed here has shown any desire for attending a course at Coleg

1 Hilda Jennings, *The private citizen in public social work* (Allen & Unwin, 1930) p. 229.

2 The Pilgrim Trust, *First Annual Report 1930-1931*, p. 5.

3 Peter Stead, *Coleg Harlech, the first fifty years* (Cardiff: University of Wales Press, 1977).

Harlech. They seem to think that Coleg Harlech has become a kind of Reformatory School, and I fail to convince them otherwise'.[1]

Another source of misunderstanding was over the question of control and supervision in work amongst the unemployed. Voluntary workers were all too conscious of the dangers of excessive supervision and control at the local level. The pattern that emerged was one in which some control passed from executives and trustees to locally-elected committees, whilst these committees remained subordinate to a wider pattern of supervision. Henry Mess described this as a 'dyarchy' in which those 'who provided premises and equipment exercised some control; as trustees they were bound to do so, . . . but . . . usually within a framework of conditions the men's clubs were free to manage the clubs they though fit'.[2] The formula was found to work smoothly and the voluntary movement could justifiably claim that by the mid-1930s many of the unemployed clubs in particular were 'self-governing and democratically controlled'. Not all outsiders were happy with this optimism and again the language used tended to create misunderstanding. Sir Wyndham Portalis' report on South Wales in 1934 concluded with regard to voluntary committees that 'generally speaking the right type of person is in control' and in so doing he indicated a concern that was very common amongst voluntary workers.[3] Could there be democracy in a situation which was open to exploitation by the wrong element? This problem was often touched on in contemporary literature. In 1932 *The Times* labour correspondent advised his readers as to how voluntary and preventive work should be organised and he stressed the need 'for associating a group of the unemployed with capacities for leadership with the promoters of the centre at the earliest moment'. This was indeed what was to happen and the voluntary movement was quite right to stress the growing democracy of the clubs as was the Pilgrim Trust Report justified in talking of the clubs having provided an 'education in democracy'.[4] *The Times* correspondent, however, was equally prophetic when, having stressed the need for 'a sense of corporate responsibility', he went on to conclude that 'natural leaders will come to the front if there is the opportunity, and what may be termed invisible oversight will ensure that men of a doubtful type are excluded. Spoon-feeding and charity do not appeal to the virile'.[5] Here again was an ambiguity in voluntary thinking. Most of the unemployed were aware that there were two spheres of leadership, two spheres of democracy and two spheres of political action. The clubs had won through to a local democracy but the major battles were being fought in a wider and more complex world.

Social workers laboured hard to establish their schemes as indigenous rather than alien creations. They were aware that notions of charity and overtones of paternalism had to be disguised and played down. In this respect they were to be hampered more than anything by

1 Letter at Coleg Harlech.

2 Henry A Mess, *Voluntary social services since 1918* (Kegan Paul, 1948) p. 47.

3 Ministry of Labour, *Report on South Wales and Monmouthshire*, Section XI, Voluntary Social Services, p. 57.

4 *Men without work*, p. 306.

5 *The Times*, 21 December 1932.

the image given to voluntary effort by the prominence within its ranks of aristocratic and titled persons. Wal Hannington loved to play with the names of those who led the voluntary movement and his stressing of the prominence of the Rt Hon E A Fitzroy, of the Rt Hon the Viscount Bledisloe and of Lieut Colonel G R Crosfield in the councils of the NCSS can have done little to recommend that organisation in the Rhondda and in Jarrow.[1] There were sincere and able social workers in the communities and an impressive professionalism was developing at the regional and national levels but there can be no doubt that voluntaryism was throughout the Depression stigmatised by its close connection with the last stages of an old-fashioned individual philanthropy in which the rich and the socially prominent bestowed favours on those less fortunate than themselves. Voluntary movements were becoming increasingly part of an official response to unemployment but they could never be very sure about how much government money would come or when it would come and this uncertainty made them dependent to a greater or lesser extent on the generosity of individual patrons. Throughout the country there were still many thousands of families, whose wealth was inherited or earned in industry, trade and the professions, who gave generously to relief schemes. It is doubtful whether many voluntary schemes could have survived without this patronage. Much of this philanthropy went unsung except in obscure annual reports and it was only one or two extrovert benefactors who made the national headlines. More than anybody it was Lady Astor who gave a bad name to philanthropy and Cliveden came to have as many unpleasant connotations in the domestic sphere as it did in foreign affairs. Tom Jones, who was to work closely with the Astors and who was described as having an instructive urge to 'tell his rich friends where their duty lies', described in detail how Lady Astor had woken up 'in the middle of the night thinking of life's inequalities', had resolved 'to adopt a Welsh village' and had immediately despatched her daughter to Rhymney with what had originally been intended as Christmas gifts for the house-guests at Cliveden. In the years that followed, Lady Astor's flair for publicity, her patronising tone and her other-worldly quality was to infuriate Labour MPs, the unemployed and sometimes social workers themselves. Apart from her emphasis on the very fact of giving, it was her moral tone which tended to stick in the gullet. Michael Astor was later to sum up the group who gathered around his mother to discuss social problems and to advise her as 'lopsided, dry and prudish, viewing life from the carefully tended parlours of their minds rather than coming out to meet it in the alleys and main streets where it was less regulated and less predictable'.[2]

That the social workers themselves were frequently embarrassed by the Lady Bountiful image given to their work was best indicated in an essay written by Henry Mess in the early 1940s. Mess, who in the 1930s had been a pioneering Director of the Tyneside Council of Social Service, admitted that many of the accusations that voluntary work was characterised by snobbishness and by a patronising attitude were correct. He maintained that 'deference to the rich and the titled is carried further in the field of voluntary social service than in most fields of national life' and he went on to deplore 'this toadying to the rich and the titled'

1 Hannington, *Distressed areas*, p. 200.

2 Thomas Jones, *Whitehall diary*, ed. Keith Middlemass (3 vols. Oxford UP, 1969) II, 159; Michael Astor, *Tribal feeling* (Murray, 1963) p. 80.

and to call for a purge of these elements.[1] Like most social workers, he could see that there was now no substitute for statutory provision, for it was only this which would remove the ambiguity inherent in a situation in which there was a giver and a receiver.

The most telling argument which the voluntary organisations were able to use in their own favour was that they were providing services and relief which nobody else would have provided and that, in particular, they were moving into communities in which many of the traditional and indigenous institutions had failed and proved inadequate and unadaptable. In *Men without work* it was strongly maintained that 'the social institutions which existed in the valleys before the depression have been unable to carry the weight which it thrust on them'.[2] It was shown that the old agencies such as the Labour Party, the trade unions and the Nonconformist denominations had found it impossible to hold their membership and to devise new activities which would appeal to the unemployed. This diagnosis was substantially correct and the historian is bound to conclude that mass unemployment seriously reduced the numerical strength of the traditional institutions. Bakke concluded that 'political group action does not rank high among the tactics adopted by the unemployed as a means for solving their problems'[3] and *The Times* correspondent noted that more and more marriages in South Wales were taking place in registry offices and that this was a symptom of 'dwindling congregations at places of worship' and 'of the large number of churches which are endeavouring to carry on without pastoral guidance'.[4] In South Wales the miners' union made valiant and perhaps unique efforts to retain its unemployed members but, in general, trade unions too experienced this sharp decline in numerical strength.

That indigenous institutions failed and to some extent languished cannot be denied but what is often forgotten is that in declining, these institutions did not lose their legitimacy. The unemployed man might no longer be an active trade unionist or an active ward-member of his Labour Party, he might well be more inclined to play billiards or go to the pictures rather than attend a prayer-meeting, but this did not mean that he totally relinquished his emotional ties with his union, his political party and his chapel. The vast majority of the unemployed were not normally activists but they retained the general values of the communities in which they lived. Throughout the Depression social workers and civil servants were to bemoan the reluctance of the unemployed to leave the distressed areas. The reasons for this were complex but one should not underestimate the extent to which it was precisely those institutions now written off as failures which had shaped that culture from which it was difficult to shift the unemployed. Those unemployed men who moved to Slough, Dagenham or Coventry immediately complained of the lack of active ward meetings, union branches and chapel-related activities.[5] This deeper pattern of loyalty

1 Mess, *Voluntary social services*, p. 209.

2 *Men without work*, p. 307.

3 Bakke, *Citizens without work*, p. 46.

4 *The Times*, 25 February 1930.

5 One Welshman who had migrated to Birmingham commented on how he missed 'the Social and Trade Union Activity' (Coleg Harlech, *10th Annual Report*, 1937).

was most concretely expressed in the reluctance of the unemployed to engage in any relief work which would rival work already being done by employed trade-unionists. This institutional loyalty was something that social workers often failed to understand. The most powerful testimony to this is found in Miss Jennings' account of the difficulties experienced in launching co-operative enterprises at Brynmawr. She tells of how often the voluntary workers came across 'closed minds' produced by 'industrial, political and denominational warfare'. What was to anger her particularly was pressure put on workers in the co-operatives by trade-unionists involved in industrial disputes but she also commented on the way in which the argument that voluntary work was 'detrimental to Trade Unionism' had its effect on 'the popular imagination'.[1] Henry Mess was also to recall this opposition from the unions, although it was his view that 'it was seldom the big leaders who objected, it was the small fry'. His contention was that most voluntary schemes carried out work which would not otherwise have been done, that men trained in the voluntary workshops would not compete with 'fully trained men' and that, 'even if there had been a small percentage of men getting into industry by such back-doors or a small percentage of work done gratis which might possibly have been done for wages, the risk and harm would have been small as against the harm of men rotting in idleness'.[2] There was always to be controversy as to how useful was relief work. The best known public debate was that concerning the early efforts at Brynmawr. In his famous broadcast of December 1932, the Prime Minister, Ramsay MacDonald, had actually singled out the efforts at Brynmawr as an exaple of what could be achieved. The immediate response of the Brynmawr Urban District Council was to ask their Clerk to write to the Prime Minister pointing out that voluntary relief work had so far done little to help the unemployed in Brynmawr. Their argument was that the relief work had employed mainly student labour and unlike local authority schemes, had not actually channelled money into the hands of the unemployed. This letter was to be given the maximum of publicity and was to occasion a great deal of anxiety amongst voluntary-workers. It was published in the *Daily Worker* in January 1933 in the hope that 'it will strengthen the determination of the workers to fight against the trickery of these charity schemes'.[3] It was later quoted in full by Hannington in *The problem of the distressed areas*. Tom Jones, who did more than any other person to establish relief schemes in South Wales, very often had doubts about what was being achieved and in a brilliant essay he parodied and satirised all that was being done by the Prince of Wales, Lady Astor, the Commissioner for Special Areas and their agents. His suggestion that everyone should be transferred out of South Wales and that the valleys be flooded, used as an industrial museum and used for bombing practice brilliantly conveyed both the sense of uselessness that many social workers must have experienced and their desire to escape from the never-ending problems presented by South Wales.[4] To the unemployed themselves the paradox was always very clear: if the

1 Jennings, *Brynmawr*, p. 198 et seq.

2 Mess, *Voluntary social services*, p. 53.

3 *The Daily Worker*, 2 January 1932.

4 Thomas Jones, 'What's wrong with South Wales' (1935) printed in *Leeks and daffodils* (Newtown: Welsh Outlook Press, 1942) pp. 89-114.

work and the training were worthwhile, of course there would be a threat to their comrades in employment; if there was no threat then they were right to question whether the work was worthwhile and the training comprehensive. Along with Henry Mess, voluntary workers argued that but for them there would be no playing fields and swimming pools and that without voluntary schemes many men, women and youths would have been faced with hours of idleness. The reality and effectiveness of these claims were, nevertheless, always susceptible to one argument more than any other, and this was the accusation that voluntary schemes, however sophisticated and professional, were ultimately only serving as diversions. In one film sponsored by the NCSS a group of unemployed miners are shown to be cynical about what voluntary schemes could do for them. One miner thought that such activity would be 'better than doing nothing' but an opponent of the suggested scheme talked of it as 'only killing time' and as not constituting 'real work'.[1] Relief work could never be 'real work'. This was the killing accusation that did more than anything to reduce the status and effectiveness of the commitment to voluntary work. In 1938 the Bishop of Llandaff, in whose diocese was to be found much of the worst distress in Wales, led a delegation to the Minister of Labour at which time he stressed the need for major political and economic initiatives. He pointed out that 'efforts are being made to help us along - splendid efforts - in the matter of social services, and various agencies are at work' but he also felt that that 'really does not get at the root of the matter. It is like bringing to a man who is sick little comforts and delicacies, grapes and comforts of that kind, all splendid things in their way, but what is the use of these when the man is in need of an operation to save his life?'.[2]

In general those who had been involved in the 'splendid efforts' of the Depression had been aware of the difficulties that had stood in their way and of those they had created themselves. Their ultimate justification was, as Henry Mess put it, that 'they would have been much worse years' but for voluntary effort.[3] By the war-years most social workers realised that they had been doing much that should have been done by statutory provision and they would have agreed with Constance Braithwaite's notion that 'the function of charity is to demonstrate the desirability and practicability of particular forms of services until such time as the State is willing to finance these services'.[4] Voluntary workers, though, were not entirely on the defensive and one does not have to look far for arguments advanced in favour of the voluntary principle. One prominent adult educationalist defended the voluntary tradition in adult education in terms that would have brought loud 'amens' from many quarters; he said of the existing pattern that 'uniformity and control must not reign here. Variety is its genius, uniformity its death, exploration and freedom

1 *Today we live* (Strand Films for NCSS, 1937). See also Donald Alexander's film *Eastern valley* for reactions to Peter Scott's co-operative venture.

2 Public Record Office, Ministry of Labour, PIN 18/38.

3 Mess, *Voluntary social services*, p. 54.

4 Constance Braithwaite, *The voluntary citizen: an enquiry into the place of philanthropy in the community* (Methuen, 1938) p. 25.

its life blood; standardisation, complacency and authority are fatal'.[1] Supporters of voluntaryism stressed its flexibility, the ease with which it could experiment and be used to deal with controversial matters, its potential for redemptive work and the way it could avoid the stigma often attached to government action. By the 1940s there was general agreement that what was needed was a fusion between the flexibility and dynamism of voluntary action and the resources and power of the State. A sensitive philanthropy could, as Constance Braithwaite argued, nicely off-set 'the defects of state action' such as 'standardisation' and the 'inadequate reflection of minority opinions'. Voluntary workers felt that society would always have some need for their vision and that, as Miss Jennings had argued, 'society gains by the social effort of the private citizen'.[2]

Lessons, however, had been learned. The Great Depression had forced governments into a new economics and, as part of this, the huge army of the unemployed had educated both government and social workers into new concepts of welfarism. The national agencies, official and voluntary, had been confronted by the reality of unemployment and by the reality of the unemployed's perception of their unemployment. In the first place the unemployed man had asserted his independence and upheld his own dignity. Unemployed clubs succeeded because they were taken over and moulded in the democratic image of their members, other relief schemes were either ignored or accepted without emotional commitment. It was made clear to social workers that in Ellen Wilkinson's words, 'a man without a job is no subject for experiments in social organisation'.[3] The unemployed, though, not only asserted their independence but also established the reality of their own social existence. The unemployed were social beings, products of a culture in which certain values of mutuality, of inter-dependence and of political radicalism were taken for granted. Voluntary workers came into the distressed communities with sympathy and with an urge to get things done but it took time for them to realise that traditional loyalties and the belief in collective values and collective action were not the outpourings of provincial, idiosyncratic and 'closed' minds but were a legitimate and profound response to the nature of modern industrial society. They were encountering a different experience and a different, not to say deeper, wisdom. As we have seen, Wight Bakke concluded that efforts to help the unemployed would be 'inadequate unless they are shaped with the purpose of restoring as nearly as possible the normal structures of societal living'. To him this necessitated an understanding of 'the customary goals towards which workers are striving, the normal conditions under which that striving is carried on and the habitual relations and practices which have grown out of the effort to reach them'.[4] That these things were only slowly and partially understood was due in part to social ignorance and distance and in part to a lack of political and social faith. The outsiders had encountered an independence born out of a different experience but one buttressed by a greater faith, not only in collective

1 Benjamin B Thomas, 'Adult education in Wales and the statutory body', *Journal of Adult Education*, XI (1938) 149.

2 Braithwaite, *Voluntary citizen*, p. 7 and Jennings, *The private citizen*, p. 229.

3 Ellen C Wilkinson, *The town that was murdered: the life story of Jarrow* (Gollancz, 1939) p. 232.

4 Bakke, *Citizens without work*, p. 305.

action for its own sake but in what that collective action could achieve. As Nye Bevan pointed out in 1933, 'there is in all ranks of the Conservative Party a deep disbelief in the capacity to get themselves out of their difficulties'. It was precisely Bevan's combination of independence and political optimism that voluntary movements could never hope to emulate.[1]

1 *Parliamentary Debates*, 27 April 1933.

www.ingramcontent.com/pod-product-compliance
Ingram Content Group UK Ltd.
Pitfield, Milton Keynes, MK11 3LW, UK
UKHW061842041026
15591UKWH00014B/870

9 780859 890434